simulation in social science
READINGS

PRENTICE-HALL INTERNATIONAL, INC.
London • *Tokyo* • *Sydney*
PRENTICE-HALL OF CANADA, LTD.

HAROLD GUETZKOW, Editor
Northwestern University

simulation in social science
READINGS

The Library
Southwestern State College
Weatherford, Oklahoma

PRENTICE-HALL, INC.,   Englewood Cliffs, N.J.

Current printing (last digit):

11   10   9   8   7   6   5   4   3   2

© 1962 by Harold Guetzkow

All rights reserved. No part of this book
may be reproduced in any form, by mimeograph
or any other means, without permission in
writing from the publishers.

Library of Congress Catalog Card No. 62-16887

PRINTED IN THE UNITED STATES OF AMERICA

81033–C

300.18
G93s

To Robert Wesner
bookman par excellence

109163

preface

This book of readings on *Simulation in Social Science* has been assembled so that the efforts to simulate complex individual and group processes might be more adequately understood by our colleagues and students—and especially by our lay friends. The volume provides source material on the use of man, man-computer, and all-computer simulation which will acquaint the reader with the recent and expanding use of simulation as a technique for experimentation and teaching in the behavioral sciences.

The readings include pieces on the use of simulation in economics, political science, psychology, and sociology. Materials are included on its employment in military and industrial operations, as well as in management activities (including those in education). The opening essay by Richard Dawson presents an overview of and orientation to the many activities in the field. The Glossary gives meanings of terms widely used in handling concepts in simulation. And for those hardy souls who find time to read further, there is a short, classified bibliography.

HAROLD GUETZKOW

acknowledgments

Simulation in Social Science was developed during the summer of 1961 with considerable aid from Richard Dawson, a graduate student in Northwestern's Program of Graduate Training and Research in Political Behavior. His introductory essay, a fine record of his understanding of simulation, was written in response to my query: "What facts about simulation would students and laymen want to know before perusing the collection of readings?" The glossary is also the product of Dawson's efforts as he worked through the jargon of a rapidly developing field. I also wish to express my gratitude to Larry A. Eberhardt, who prepared the Index for this volume.

Without many opportunities in years past to nurture ideas about simulation one could not hope to develop a book of readings during a single summer. In my work at the University of Michigan I was given the opportunity to work in experimentation with contrived groups, and later I gained first-hand experience in simulation as founder of the Social Science Laboratory of the Graduate School of Industrial Administration at the Carnegie Institute of Technology. My year at the Center for Advanced Study in the Behavioral Sciences enabled me to concern myself more directly with theoretical problems involving the use of man-computer forms of simulation. Since 1957, my work in the simulation of inter-nation relations at Northwestern University has been supported by the Carnegie Corporation and by contracts with the Air Force Office of Scientific Research (Contract No. AF 49 [638]-742) and the U. S. Navy Purchasing Office of the Naval Ordnance Test Station, China Lake, California (Contract No. N123 [60530] 25875A).

This collection of source materials was undertaken as a part of my activities as chairman of a Seminar on Simulation of Human Organizational Systems, which was made possible by the Group Psychology

Branch of the Office of Naval Research (Contract No. Nonr.-1228 [22]). To these groups and institutions, and to those who expedited these opportunities—to Donald Marquis, Herbert Simon, Richard Snyder, and Ralph Tyler in the academic world; to William Marvel, Charles Hutchinson, Herman Sander, Thomas Milburn, and Luigi Petrullo in the world of foundations and government—may I acknowledge my deepest thanks.

My most important debt, of course, is to the twenty-five gentlemen, who have been so scholarly as to have produced these articles and so gracious as to allow their publication in this volume. Their names and present institutional affiliations follow.

contributors and institutional affiliations

Robert Abelson: Department of Psychology, Yale University.

Jack A. Adams: Aviation Psychology Laboratory, Department of Psychology, The University of Illinois.

William C. Biel: The System Development Corporation.

Robert L. Chapman: Training and Simulation Department, The Ramo-Wooldridge Division of Thompson-Ramo-Wooldridge Corporation.

K. J. Cohen: The Graduate School of Industrial Administration, Carnegie Institute of Technology

James S. Coleman: Department of Sociology, Johns Hopkins University.

Richard M. Cyert: The Graduate School of Industrial Administration, Carnegie Institute of Technology.

Richard E. Dawson: Department of Political Science, Northwestern University.

Justin H. Dickins: The Port of New York Authority.

William R. Dill: The Graduate School of Industrial Administration, Carnegie Institute of Technology.

William M. Evan: School of Industrial Management, Massachusetts Institute of Technology.

Norman Frederiksen: Educational Testing Service.

Carl I. Hovland: Formerly with the Department of Psychology, Yale University, deceased.

Norman Jennings: The Port of New York Authority.

John L. Kennedy: Department of Psychology, Princeton University.

A. A. Kuehn: The Graduate School of Industrial Administration, Carnegie Institute of Technology.

Donald G. Malcolm: Operations Research Incorporated.

M. H. Miller: The Graduate School of Business, The University of Chicago.

Allen Newell: The RAND Corporation and the Carnegie Institute of Technology.

Guy H. Orcutt: Department of Economics, The University of Wisconsin.

Ithiel de Sola Pool: The Center for International Studies, The Massachusetts Institute of Technology.

R. P. Rich: Applied Physics Laboratory, The Johns Hopkins University.

T. A. Van Wormer: The School of Business, Washington State University.

P. R. Winters: The Graduate School of Industrial Administration, Carnegie Institute of Technology.

Morris Zelditch, Jr.: Department of Sociology, Stanford University.

table of contents

1. simulation in the social sciences

RICHARD E. DAWSON
Northwestern University

Simulation is of increasing importance to social and be-havioral scientists. The term appears frequently in a wide variety of social science literature and in reports of social science experiments. Earlier, the term was used almost exclusively in the discourses of various branches of engineering. In recent years, however, the use of the term and a more explicit use of the method it designates have spread into military science, industrial engineering, business and management training and research, economics, psychology, political science and sociology.

The current employment of simulation in social science is related to the development of system analysis, the social psychological study of groups, the use of more formal models, the employment of various mathematical techniques and the availability of high speed electronic computers. Simulation, as the study of systems through the construc-tion and operation of models, has followed the use of these different but closely related techniques into the social sciences. This essay will discuss the meaning, types, uses, values and problems of simulation as a tool for research, training and teaching in the social sciences.

I. WHAT IS SIMULATION?

The term *simulation* has also been used in a variety of different, yet closely related, senses. Like other terms currently used in social science literature, it has a technical meaning and two or more popular meanings. In popular usage the term sometimes refers to the assump-

Published here for the first time with the permission of the author.

tion of the appearance of something without having its reality. For instance, electric light may be termed simulated sunlight. It possesses many of the illuminating properties of sunlight but is not actually sunlight. In other instances, simulation refers more specifically to the assumption of false appearances for the sake of deception. This second usage of the term has been adopted in the biological sciences. *A Dictionary of Scientific Terms* defines simulation as: "Assumption of features or structures intended to deceive enemies, as forms of leaf and stick insects, and all varieties of protective coloration."[1] As currently used to depict a method of research in the social sciences, the term is employed without the connotation of deception.

Simulation is certainly not a new device. Its use probably precedes recorded history. In a very broad sense of the term, it can be argued that man has been simulating objects ever since he first began to draw and carve representations of objects on tree trunks and on the stone walls of cliffs and caves. In this very broad meaning of the word any construction of a "model," whether symbolic (pictorial, verbal, mathematical) or physical might be termed simulation. In this sense the classical dialogues of Plato, the 15th century art of Leonardo Da Vinci and the abstract art of the twentieth century might all be termed simulation, inasmuch as they are attempts to portray or reproduce by means of words, stone or canvas their authors' conception of various aspects of human life or physical objects.

The earliest practical use of simulation was the construction of physical models of real objects, particularly for work in designing tools and other objects. As Conway *et al.* point out: "Simulation has for a good many years been a useful device to the designer. He has tank-tested hull shapes, tested airfoils and scale models of airframes in wind-tunnels, and built pilot versions of chemical processing plants."[2] The construction of a model of or simulation of the real object, permits the designer to test the whole or specified aspects of the object he wants to build on the replica and thus avoid mistakes and waste in the construction of the real object.

In the general, more popular use of the term, all model building might be termed simulation. But we are interested in a more specific meaning when referring to the use of simulation as a research, train-

---

[1] I. F. Henderson and W. D. Henderson, *A Dictionary of Scientific Terms* (Edinburgh: Oliver and Boyd Ltd, 1960), p. 497.

[2] R. W. Conway, B. M. Johnson and W. L. Maxwell, "Some Problems of Digital Systems Simulation," *Management Science,* VI, No. 1 (1959), 92.

ing and teaching device in the study of human systems. The social or behavioral scientist is primarily concerned with the study of psychological and social processes. Simulation, as a social science research technique, refers to the construction and manipulation of an *operating* model, that model being a physical or symbolic representation of all or some aspects of a social or psychological process. Simulation, for the social scientist, is the building of an operating model of an individual or group process and experimenting on this replication by manipulating its variables and their interrelationships.

II. SIMULATIONS ARE MODELS

Since simulation is so closely related to the construction of and the use of models, it seems appropriate to discuss briefly the use of models in social science. A model of something—a physical object, a living organism or a social system—is a physical or symbolic representation of that object, designed to incorporate or reproduce those features of the real object that the researcher deems significant for his research problem. The term model, as used here, refers to a scientific tool. It does not connote that the representation is an ideal or a "good model," worthy of emulation. Brody points out that "Developing a model involves abstracting from reality those components and relationships which are hypothesized as crucial to what is being modeled."[3] The choice of essential aspects of the reality being modeled depends upon the purposes for which the model is being constructed. In some cases—like a model ship to be displayed in a bottle—the object of the model construction is to reproduce as many of the details of the real object as possible, only on a smaller scale. In other cases—like the hydraulic model of an economic system,[4]— whether the model has the physical appearance of the real object is of little importance. The important factor is that the components and variables being investigated through the model respond in a manner comparable to that of the behavior of the real system.

---

[3] Richard A. Brody, "Political Games for Model Construction in International Relations," The Program of Graduate Training and Research in International Relations, Department of Political Science, Northwestern University, June, 1961 (unpublished mimeo); to be published in Guetzkow *et al., The Use of Simulation for Teaching and Research in International Relations* (Englewood Cliffs, N.J.: Prentice-Hall, Inc., 1963), p. 2.

[4] Irving Fisher, *Mathematical Investigations in the Theory of Value and Prices* (New Haven: Yale University Press, 1925), p. 44.

Models can be constructed in several different media. Until recently nearly all description and analysis in the social sciences has been verbal, pictorial or diagrammatic. Plato's *Republic* and Toynbee's *Study of History* use verbal models for the description and analysis of social systems. Economists and sociologists have made much use of pictorial or diagrammatic models in the form of supply and demand charts and organizational authority flow charts.

As the social sciences have developed and the social scientists have increased their understanding of the phenomena they study, it has been possible to translate physical, verbal and pictorial models into mathematical models. In the construction of mathematical models, properties of the real objects or systems are abstracted by measurement and expressed in a set of mathematical equations, as Simon has done in his *Models of Man.*[5] Quantitative measures supplement the qualitative distinctions of verbal and pictorial models, and general descriptions of the relationships between variables are replaced by more precise equations. Before mathematical models can be developed, the relationships among units and variables must be structured so that the latter correspond to the rules of relationship which constitute the mathematical methods being used. When appropriate mathematical models can be constructed, the scientist has a powerful tool to aid him in understanding the behavior of the object or system he is investigating. The abstractness of the symbol system in a mathematical model makes possible the recognition of similarities and congruences between various models and thus between the realities they represent. Many of the simulation exercises used in social sciences are done wholly or in part with mathematical models.[6]

As was intimated above, simulation as employed by social science makes use of models constructed in such a way that they may become operative or functioning. Operating models are representations of

[5] H. A. Simon, *Models of Man* (New York: John Wiley & Sons, Inc., 1957).

[6] For more extensive discussion of the relationship between models and simulation see Brody, *op. cit.;* Martin Shubik, "Simulation, Its Uses and Potential, Part I" (Unpublished Mimeo), Anticipation Project Expository and Development Paper, No. 3, General Electric Corp., Operations Research and Synthesis Consulting Service, May 4, 1959; and Guy H. Orcutt, "Simulation of Economic Systems," *The American Economic Review,* L, No. 5 (1960), 893-907. For a general discussion of the use of models in social science see Anatol Rapoport, "Uses and Limitations of Mathematical Models in Social Sciences," and May Brodbeck, "Models, Meaning, and Theories," both in *Symposium on Sociological Theory,* Llewellyn Gross, ed. (Evanston, Illinois: Row, Peterson and Company, 1959).

behaving systems that attempt to reproduce processes in action. As such, operating models provide information about variable, component and relationship changes within a system over time. These models or parts of them can be expressed in physical, chemical and biological media and through verbal, pictorial or mathematical languages. In most instances operating models will involve combinations of these several modes of representation.

III. PURPOSES FOR WHICH SIMULATION IS EMPLOYED

As the above discussion has suggested, simulation can be used by social scientists for a wide variety of purposes. Basically the social scientist simulates to investigate and to learn about the behavior of individual and group processes. Such learning may be used for at least four very useful purposes: (1) design; (2) the development of a body of knowledge; (3) training; and (4) teaching.

To aid in the designing of new and improving the design of old materials or systems is probably the oldest use to which simulation has been put. It has been widely used for design purposes in the physical sciences, especially in engineering, for some time. The experiments with aircraft models in wind tunnels illustrate how simulation is useful in choosing between alternative designs. By manipulating the pressure and direction of the wind, as well as size, structure and materials of the model plane, in the simulated situation, the experimenter is able to learn something of how various designs would work under different conditions in the real atmosphere. This same principle is quite useful in designing and refining various social systems. For instance, in the simulation of an air defense system, reported on in this book by Conway *et al.,* the researchers seek to experiment with the system in simulated situations to learn how the system can be best designed to cope with real problems.

Simulation is also useful in helping the social scientist build a body of knowledge concerning various social or individual systems. The object of science is the formulation of theories that explain and predict behavior. Simulation is a very useful device for the exploration of verbal theories and the testing of hypotheses. In many instances, especially in the study of social and psychological phenomena, it is undesirable or even impossible to conduct experiments upon real systems. By successfully simulating the significant variables, it is possible to explore such phenomena by experimenting with the simulated system.[7]

Simulation has value as a teaching device. The hydraulic model of an economic system portrays quite vividly the general nature of a complex economic system, an analytical system often too "abstract" for many to understand through verbal description. Guetzkow's internation simulation and the Carnegie Tech Management Game are used to help teach college students about the behavior of complex social systems by having the students make decisions, handle data and experience consequences in the simulated systems, comparable to those which occur in the real system.

The training purposes of simulation are closely related to the teaching functions. In teaching, the student is presumed to learn about the system. In training, it is hoped that the trainees will learn how to fill various operating roles in the real system by participating in comparable roles in simulated situations. As Orcutt observes of the training function of simulation, ". . . the trainee is able to get some feel of what he would experience in the real situation and some indication of the likely outcome of various actions and responses on his part."[8] Jack Adams' article on "Some Considerations in the Design and Use of Dynamic Flight Simulators" in this volume discusses problems in the use of simulation for training purposes.

IV. THE VOCABULARY OF SIMULATION

A variety of simulation techniques has been developed and employed by social scientists, and a number of terms are currently in use designating different approaches, purposes and techniques. Among the more frequent terms used in the social science literature in connection with simulation are man-machine simulation, gaming, Monte Carlo techniques, digital computer simulation, analog computer simulation, machine simulation and real-time simulation. At present, there is disagreement and sometimes even confusion as to the meanings and distinctions between some of these terms; especially concerning the relationship between simulation, gaming and Monte Carlo techniques. Commenting on the use of these terms Thomas and Deemer say:

---

[7] For a discussion of the use of simulation for theory exploration and hypothesis testing see Harold Guetzkow, "Simulation in the Study of Inter-Nation Relations," in this volume.

[8] Orcutt, *op. cit.,* 895.

It is difficult to agree on a common terminology for current operational gaming, however, because its antecedents suggest diverse usages. Traditional war gaming, Monte Carlo computation, parlor games, and the von Neumann-Morgenstern theory of games all have contributed ideas and words. Beyond this historically inspired confusion, diverse local usages spring up at individual establishments to meet the needs of particular problems.[9]

Although Thomas and Deemer are speaking more specifically to the field of operational gaming in operations research, their comments are applicable to the current situation in social science simulation.

Some writers attempt to make clear distinctions between simulation, gaming and Monte Carlo techniques.[10] Others fuse the techniques, either regarding them as synonymous or seeing one or two of the processes as subcategories of the other one or two.[11] Distinctions between simulation (or man-machine simulation), gaming and Monte Carlo techniques have been suggested based on the general purposes to be served by the process,[12] the role of human beings vs. machines,[13] the element of competition,[14] the tightness or looseness of interactions within the simulated system, and the type of language in which the simulation process is expressed.[15] Although there are values to be gained from classifying different types of simulation procedures and related techniques according to any of these criteria, these distinctions are generally offered in connection with the solution of specified problems in particular areas of concern. When one attempts to apply these categorical distinctions between simulation, gaming and Monte Carlo techniques to a wider range of problems, they tend to become unnecessarily restrictive. Given the general disagreement in the literature as to how classifications should be made, the ambi-

---

[9] Clayton J. Thomas and Walter L. Deemer, Jr., "The Role of Operational Gaming in Operations Research," *Operation Research,* V, No. 1 (1957), 3.

[10] See Thomas and Deemer, *op. cit.,* and Martin Shubik, "Simulation of Industry," *The American Economic Review,* L, No. 5 (1960), 910-912.

[11] See Charles D. Flagle, "Simulation Techniques," in *Operations Research and Systems Engineering,* Charles D. Flagle *et al.,* eds. (Baltimore: The Johns Hopkins Press, 1960), p. 446; R. P. Rich, "Simulation as an Aid in Model Building," *Operations Research,* III (1955), 15-19; N. M. Smith, Jr., "A Rationale for Operational Gaming," Paper presented to 8th National Meeting of the Operations Research Society, Ottawa, Canada, January 10, 1956; and R. A. Brody, *op. cit.*

[12] Shubik, "Simulation Its Uses and Potential, Part I," *op. cit.*

[13] Brody, *op. cit.,* p. 6.

[14] E. W. Martin, "Teaching Executives Via Simulation," *Business Horizons,* II, No. 2 (1959), 101.

[15] Thomas and Deemer, *op. cit.,* 4-7.

guity of some of these classification schemes, and the young but rapidly developing state of simulation in the social sciences, it seems most useful to regard simulation as a general term referring to constructing and operating on a model that replicates behavioral processes; gaming as a type of simulation; and Monte Carlo techniques as a process used in some simulation operations.

It is rewarding to discuss the terms which have been applied in describing simulations. Some social scientists distinguish between simulations which are conducted entirely on machines (pure-machine), and simulations which make use of human decision makers with or without the additional use of machines (man-machine or all-man simulation).

Pure-Machine Simulation. It seems useful to identify two subgroups within the pure-machine simulation category; (a) physical analog simulation—those operations using some sort of physical model; and, (b) those simulations employing only a mathematical model. In physical analog simulation, problems are solved by manipulating parts of one physical system constructed as a model of another physical or analytical system. The Rich piece in this book gives an example of a simple physical analog simulator.

In the nonphysical analog simulation the model being operated on is constructed in symbolic form. The model is operated by manipulating the various symbols and programs which replicate the variables and components of the system. In most cases this operation is carried out on a digital electronic computer. The Orcutt, Coleman, Hovland, and Pool and Abelson simulations discussed in this book are all examples of this type of simulation.

Simulations Including Human Actors. Simulations in which human decision-makers act and interact within the simulated system are currently used by social scientists, especially for training and teaching purposes. The Chapman *et al.,* Guetzkow, Cohen *et al.,* Frederiksen, and Zelditch-Evan articles in this volume discuss this type of simulation. Both what is labeled "man-machine simulation" and those simulations commonly called "gaming" fall in this category. In man-machine simulation and games both the actions of human actors (participating as system decision-makers, not as experimenters) and computing machines simulate a social or psychological system. This type of simulation may be used to train the participants to serve in various capacities such as top management positions, to teach students about the operations of some social system and to help the scholar investigate behavior in a real system by manipulating activities in a simulated system. The AMA Top Management Game[16] is an example of a game or man-machine simulation of business situations developed to train executives in the making of top level decisions. The Northwestern inter-nation simulation and the Carnegie Tech Management Game reported in this book are examples of man-machine simulation or gaming, used both to teach students about inter-nation and business systems and to investigate hypotheses concerning international relations and business organizations. In the RAND simulation of an air defense system, reported on in this book by Chapman *et al.,* the man-machine simulation was employed to help the researchers learn about the performance of an air defense organization.

Games. Since the term "game" or "gaming" is often used in describing some simulations in which human participants serve as decision-makers acting within the system, it seems desirable to describe briefly the development of those operations labeled gaming. Although some writers maintain that there is a distinction between simulation and gaming, this writer does not consider simulation and gaming to be two separate techniques. He considers gaming to be a term sometimes applied to some simulations in which human actors participate within the simulated system, generally in a competitive situation.

E. W. Martin, Jr., defines a game as "a technical term denoting a simulation in which the results for one group depend on the actions of their competitors."[17] Martin Shubik, who distinguishes between simulation and gaming, suggests that in gaming the human decision makers learn from "playing." "When a model (a man-machine model) is used for gaming the individuals in the system are presumed to learn from the play."[18] Teaching, however, is not the only function served by the man-machine simulations used in gaming, as was pointed out above. J. M. Kibbee says of one type of gaming, "Any business game could be used for some form of research; the obverse of the coin is that any simulation could be used for training."[19]

There are three main streams of gaming of interest to social scien-

[16] F. M. Ricciardi *et al., Top Management Decision Simulation: The AMA Approach* (New York: American Management Association, Inc., 1958).

[17] Martin, *loc. cit.*

[18] Shubik, *op. cit.,* 19.

[19] J. M. Kibbee, "Management Control Simulation," in *Management Control Systems,* Donald G. Malcolm *et al.,* eds. (New York: John Wiley and Sons, Inc., 1960), p. 304.

tists: war gaming, business or management gaming and political gaming. The first of these gaming devices to be developed was war gaming, which can be traced back many centuries—possibly to the ancient game of chess. War games for purposes of military training and analysis were developed during the nineteenth century, and they were employed by both sides in the two World Wars. The Naval War College has defined war games as "a generic term describing the means for simulating the play of systematic strategic or tactical operations of opposing forces. It may include twosided board maneuvers, chart maneuvers, electronic maneuver board games, tactical games, or strategic war games."[20] Both business and political games trace their genesis to the military use of the technique. The recent application of gaming to the problems of political science and management science has been stimulated by the use of mathematical formalizations and social laboratory techniques in the study of social and psychological phenomena, and by the development of high speed electronic computers.

Business and management games are now being used by some large corporations in the training and selection of management personnel. The first important such game to be developed was the AMA Top Management Decision Game, developed by the American Management Association in 1956.[21] In more recent years the use of management and business games has spread to academic institutions, where they are used both for teaching and research purposes. In addition to teaching the techniques of management and business operation, management games have potential for research in economic systems, organizational theory, psychology, industrial relations and problems of production and marketing.[22]

Political games, generally simulating international situations, have been developed in several academic and research institutions in the past few years. The earliest attempts at formulating political games were made by the RAND Corporation starting about 1954. Their work grew out of RAND's earlier work with war games.[23] Later,

---

[20] "Brief History of War Gaming," The United States War College, Part IV.

[21] For an extensive discussion of management games see Kalman J. Cohen and Eric Rhenman, "The Role of Management Games in Education and Research," *Management Science*, VII, No. 2 (1961), 131-166.

[22] See Kalman J. Cohen *et al.,* "The Carnegie Tech Management Game," in this volume.

[23] Social Science Division, "Experimental Research on Political Gaming" (Santa Monica: RAND Corp., RAND report P-1540-RC, Nov. 10, 1958).

political games were developed at Northwestern University and then at M. I. T.[24] These games have been used for teaching and research purposes. It would seem, however, that they could also be employed for the training of decision makers and for policy formulation analysis.

In addition to terms that point out differences in the degree to which men and/or machines are involved in a simulation, two other terms are widely used in describing the differences in the time dimension and in the extent to which detailed mechanisms are supplemented by stochastic representation. These may now be presented in concluding this section on the types and techniques of simulation.

Real-Time Simulation. One of the significant advantages of many of the simulation processes is their ability to replicate years of activity in a very short period of time or to slow down time for detailed study of specific situations. In some simulation situations, however, especially those used for training purposes, it is advantageous for the simulation to be carried out in ordinary clock time. That is, the simulated activity must take as long as the real activity it is replicating. Real-time simulation is especially useful in simulators used to train persons for positions where prompt, accurate decisions are at a premium.

The Monte Carlo Method. Another technique incorporated in the operation of some simulations is the Monte Carlo method. The name *Monte Carlo* is given to the process of simulating with models that include probability distributions. The Monte Carlo method is defined by W. E. Alberts as "a computational method or technique of introducing data of a random or probabilistic nature into a model. Its purpose is to reproduce data in the same manner as would occur in a real life situation."[25] In some simulation situations in which a large number of variables are involved and in which the value of the variables and components is not constant, it is necessary to model the behavior of the system in probability terms. The Monte Carlo method is employed in such instances. Daniel D. McCracken says of this method:

> The Monte Carlo method, in general, is used to solve problems which depend in some important way upon probability—problems where physical experimentation is impracticable and the creation of

[24] See Lincoln P. Bloomfield and Norman J. Padelford, "Three Experiments in Political Gaming," *The American Political Science Review,* LIII (1959), 1105-1115.

[25] W. E. Alberts, "Report to the Eighth A. I. I. E. National Convention on the Systems Simulation Symposium," in *Report of Systems Simulation Symposium,* ed. D. G. Malcolm (Baltimore: Waverly Press, Inc., 1958), p. 4.

an exact formula is impossible. Often the process we wish to study consists of a long sequence of steps, each of which involves probability, as for instance the travels of the neutron through matter. We can write formulas for the probabilities at each collision, but we are often not able to write anything useful for the probabilities for the entire sequence.[26]

The simulation of peak hour operations in a bus terminal, reported on in this book by Jennings and Dickins, is an example of a use of the Monte Carlo method in simulation.

V. ADVANTAGES AND PROBLEMS IN SIMULATION

Up to this point we have discussed what simulation is, types and techniques of simulation, and the general purposes for which it can be used. Simulation is, like other research techniques, merely a tool, and only one of many available to the social scientist. It is not a magical cure-all for the study of all problems faced by social scientists. It must be evaluated against other research techniques. These criteria may be used in making an evaluation: (1) Applicability: Will the technique adequately solve the problems involved in the research or training exercise? (2) Cost: Are the costs in terms of time, money, equipment required and effort expended less than those for any other technique yielding comparable results? (3) Simplicity and communicability: Is it the least complex and most comprehensible technique, considering the persons who might be using it and those to whom the results might be communicated?

One of the most significant advantages of simulation is that it permits the experimenter to study process in ways that nature prohibits. The simulation can be run many times with the values of the parameters being modified between runs and the changes in outputs observed. This makes possible the effective study of operating models containing many different components, variables and interrelationships. The experimenter, in short, exercises a great amount of control through which he can study and evaluate outcomes resulting from a variety of alternative conditions and relationships. Conway, Johnson and Maxwell sum up this advantage: "Simulation is often described as a means of incorporating a fourth dimension—time—in what have previously of necessity been static methods of analysis."[27]

---

[26] Daniel D. McCracken, "The Monte Carlo Method," *Scientific American,* 192, No. 5 (1955), 94.

[27] Conway *et al., op. cit.,* p. 95.

Simulation also permits the researcher, teacher or trainer to compress or expand real time. He can simulate the operations of a system over a period of years in a matter of minutes, or he can slow down the process so that he can more carefully analyze or demonstrate what is going on in specific areas. In other situations the simulation can be used to reproduce real time.

Experimenting with a simulated system, instead of the real system, permits the social scientist to study problems that would be impractical or altogether impossible to study in real life. It is impossible for a political scientist studying international relations to experiment with the real inter-nation system of decision-makers, capabilities and organizations, manipulating variables like nuclear weapons to see what results such changes might have on international tensions. However, when significant aspects of the inter-nation system are simulated by physical analogs, mathematical formulas and/or human decision-makers the variables in the model can be manipulated and properties concerning the real system may be inferred. The ability to experiment in this fashion is particularly useful in the social sciences because moral and physical factors often prohibit experimenting with real people and real social systems. Helmer and Rescher call experimentation on simulated models "pseudo-experimentation." Speaking of the value of this process they comment, "Generally it may be said that in many cases judicious pseudo-experimentation may effectively annul the oft-regretted infeasibility of carrying out experiments proper in the social sciences by providing an acceptable substitute which, moreover, has been tried and proved in the applied physical sciences."[28]

Many simulation processes are relatively free from complex mathematics, making them more widely comprehensible than other more complex systems of formal mathematical analysis. The lack of dependency upon complex mathematical analysis not only has the advantage of making simulation comprehensible to the mathematically unsophisticated, but it can also be used in studying situations where mathematical methods capable of considering all of the desired factors are not available.

The central problem inherent in all simulation processes, and in all model building as well, is that of adequate reproduction of the real system. In simulation the researcher, teacher or trainer is trying

---

[28] Olaf Helmer and Nicholas Rescher, "On the Epistemology of the Inexact Sciences," *Management Science*, VI, No. 1 (1959), 49.

to learn or teach about a real system by working with a model of it. If the simulator does not validly model the necessary attributes of the real system, the results found in solving problems in the simulated environment cannot successfully indicate the behavior of the real system. This means that the researcher must know a great deal about the real system before he can presume to simulate it, and that he must have reliable means (mathematical, physical or human) of reproducing it. If the replication of the system and the means of operating it are not valid, the experimenter will find the use of simulation dysfunctional rather than useful.

One of the liabilities in using simulation is its high cost. Because simulation generally requires the use of large machines and/or a number of trained participants, the cost of simulation is often quite high. Cost in most instances, however, is a relative consideration. The cost of a simulation operation for the solution of a problem must be evaluated against both the cost and the results of using other techniques. For a discussion of the relative values and cost of simulation and other relevant techniques in the field of industrial engineering, see the Malcolm article in this volume. In some instances it might be decided that the cost of simulation prohibits its use and other less costly and/or less satisfactory techniques must be employed. In other situations, relative costliness cannot be considered because simulation is the only acceptable way to handle the problem.

Simulation is a useful tool when the researcher knows enough about the real system or process adequately to reproduce its behavior in an operating model, and when the problem cannot be solved successfully by simpler techniques. The user of simulation must also be careful in selecting the best type of simulation process (pure-machine, man-machine, physical analog, Monte Carlo, and so on) for the specific problem he seeks to investigate.

VI. CONCLUSION

Simulation, although a relatively new tool for the social sciences, has already proven useful for training and research concerning human organizations and psychological and social processes. As this essay and the readings that follow suggest, social or behavioral scientists have, in the past several years, begun to use simulation for a wide range of purposes. The increasingly frequent mention of the term and its use in the social science literature indicate that the technique has been found to be useful, especially for teaching, training and the generation of research hypotheses. All of this suggests an increase in the employment of simulation in the future. As the proficiency and availability of electronic computers increases, as more empirical data become available to the social scientist, as mathematical and socio-psychological techniques are improved and as the social scientist continues in his emphasis upon the study of human systems and processes, it seems reasonable to assume that the popularity and usefulness of simulation will increase.

2. computer simulation of thinking

CARL I. HOVLAND
Yale University

It is commonplace in the history of science for developments in one field of knowledge to have profound effects on other related areas. The dramatic influence of advances in atomic physics on biology, genetics, and medicine is a good case in point. We are currently witnessing a similar phenomenon in the repercussions of high speed computer technology on research in the behavioral sciences. The initial impact came from the computational efficiency of these devices which permitted calculations formerly prohibitive in terms of time and effort. A more recent and less direct effect has been in stimulating machine-like methods of analysis of human thought and behavior through simulation on high speed computers. It is these newer techniques and their applicability to psychological problems that is the topic of the present paper.

The analogy between the high speed computer and human thinking has long been noted. We frequently see the Univacs, Johniacs, Illiacs referred to in the popular press as "giant brains" or "thinking machines." In most uses of high speed computers, however, there is an attempt to attain objectives beyond the scope of human capabilities, either because of their speed or their extensive storage capacity (called, interestingly enough, their "memory"). But in the investigations I shall be describing, the utilization is quite different. Here we are primarily concerned with the use of computing machines to simulate in exact fashion the way a human solves a problem. Both human weaknesses, such as limited and fallible memory, and strengths, such as the ability to choose an efficient solution out of

Reprinted from *The American Psychologist,* 15 (1960), 687-693. With the permission of the American Psychological Association.

innumerable alternatives, must be represented. We say that we can simulate human problem solving when we are able to specify both the prior information a human possesses and the sequence of steps by which he utilizes this information in the solution of the problem. We are then able to set up a computing machine to carry out this same sequence of operation.

Those familiar with the operation of high speed computers will readily understand the way in which simulation proceeds. Just as in ordinary operations of a computer, one gives the machine a set of "instructions" to execute. These constitute a "program." In arithmetical operations these are sentences like the following: "square the product of the first and second number," "store the product in memory," "compare the first and second number," "select the larger of the two numbers compared." Or such instructions as "find the number of dollars paid to the individual last month," "add to this amount the number of dollars earned this month," and so forth. The machine then executes each of these instructions through an intricate electronic system, printing out its answers on an electric typewriter. Sequences of instructions can then solve the most complicated numerical problems, such as making out a payroll with each individual working different numbers of hours, at different wage rates, with advance payments to some workers, with different deductions for subscriptions to health and accident insurance, different income tax credits, and so forth. The nub of the simulation problem involves the use of similar types of "programs" of "instructions" to the machine in order to reproduce the steps an individual goes through in thinking out the solution to a difficult problem. One specifies the steps the individual uses by stating them in an unambiguous way so that a computing machine is able to carry them out. These may be instructions like "store the answer to the last problem," "determine whether you have stored in memory any similar problems," "if so, what are the differences between the past problem and the present problem," "see if applying Rule a will convert the old problem into the new one," and "apply Rule b" to convert the answer to the former problem into the solution to the present one. Thus the computer can be given information which is exactly equivalent to that of the human problem solver, as well as a specification of the way the human goes about processing that information to reach a solution.

The obvious point is that if we can be precise enough about a process to describe it in terms which can be programed and executed by a machine, we indeed know quite a bit about that process. And if we can specify singly each of the subprocesses involved, we can determine the effects of combinations of them and of variations in order of execution of the steps. The outcomes are almost impossible to foresee without actually carrying out the combinations and variations.

Let me begin by giving a concrete example of the new techniques, namely, simulation of the solving of geometry problems. We certainly think of the solving of theorems in Euclidian geometry by a high school sophomore as constituting a clear-cut example of intelligent human behavior. But Gelernter and Rochester (1958) of the International Business Machines Company have now successfully developed a program whereby a high speed computer is able to solve many of the theorems in Euclid's geometry, for example, that the diagonals of a parallelogram bisect one another. A human learner who tries to solve such a problem has usually been taught a series of fundamental principles, or axioms, together with a set of rules for inferring relationships by which the basic symbols in the system may be manipulated. He is then asked to prove a new theorem. He tries to find a way of transforming and combining previous axioms through the set of rules until he achieves the proof of the new theorem. Typically he starts out in rather routine fashion, then has a flash of insight as to a possible means of solution, and then methodically tests the adequacy of the solution. The geometry computing machine is set up to operate in an analogous fashion. It is given a set of basic formulas and axioms, together with rules as to possible ways of manipulating them in order to form new theorems. The new theorem is then presented to the machine to prove. The machine is equipped with a number of rules of thumb for possible ways of solving problems. For example, it is instructed that if the proposition to be proved involves parallel lines and equality of angles, there is a good chance that it may be useful to try the theorem: "If two parallel lines are intersected by a third line, the opposite interior angles are equal." This instruction constitutes a short-cut which often works well but is by no means sure to be of value. Successful solution typically involves setting up a series of subgoals which are then worked on in succession. For example, in the problem cited earlier the machine ascertains that it can solve the theorem if it can establish the fact that the distance from one corner of the base of the parallelogram to the point of intersection must equal the distance from the intersection to the opposite corner of the parallelogram. This is then a subgoal, which in turn can be proved if the triangle formed by the bisecting lines and one of the sides of the parallelogram is equal to the triangle formed by the opposite side and the corresponding bisects. A device is incorporated into the computer which makes constructions and measures lines and angles. This operates by means of coordinate geometry. Once the sequence of subgoals leads from the initial axioms to the theorem to be proved, the machine routinely tests the accuracy of the proof. This it can do in an exhaustive manner, since once one has a possible proof, checking it is largely clerical. The chief problem is to find a possible method of proceeding, out of the almost infinite number of alternatives. It is here that the short-cut methods operate. They permit the use of likely and plausible methods of solution, just the way a clever high school student would proceed. Once the proof has been verified, the machine prints QED. Throughout the entire operation the machine prints out on paper a complete tracing of the steps it tries; this is analogous to an individual's account of the way he solves a problem in geometry. Some of the machine's failures in finding proofs closely resemble those made by beginning geometry students.

It will be noted that the methods of solution built into the computer closely resemble those used by humans solving similar problems. Let me again call attention to the fact that in this way they differ from the usual uses of high speed computers which methodically go through every possible solution in a deliberate way. The complete methods guarantee that if there is a solution it will be found, although an extraordinary number of trials may be required. Solutions of this type are referred to as "algorithms." These are used here to check proofs. In contrast, finding a possible solution is facilitated by short-cuts and rules of thumb programed into the machine. In this way it simulates a human subject in making leaps in the solution and trying out schemes which have been successful in the past, rather than exhaustively trying out each possible alternative. Mathematicians call these short-cut solutions "heuristics."

One may wonder whether we have gained anything by the simulation, since we initially derive processes from study of how students work and then program into the computer their ways of proceeding. In fact, at the outset, we may operate in a somewhat circular fashion —that is, we may only get out of the machine what we put into it. But as one proceeds, new combinations are tested which could not have been predicted from the individual steps. Some results, although strictly determined by the processes programed, are impossible to foresee because so many complex operations interact in the final solution. One can find out the effect of increased complexity of problems, and then determine with human subjects whether the order of difficulty is the same that would be predicted from the computer's information processing routines. In this way one is constantly working back and forth from experiments with human subjects to simulation on the computing machine. Furthermore one frequently finds that one must make assumptions about certain steps in the process to get the computer to execute its program correctly. Here the simulation comes first and suggests later experiments with human subjects.

The geometry machine just described involves solving problems rather than learning how to solve them, in the sense that the computer would solve the same problem in the same way on a second trial. Humans, of course, do learn and improve through practice. So the interesting task is to build into the computer this capability as well. Simulation of learning is one of the most interesting potential applications of computer simulation techniques, since the ability to learn is one of the clearcut differences between human and machine performance. A number of different types of learning are currently being simulated. The first involves stimulus-response learning. It is rather simple to simulate this type of learning with rewards ("reinforcements") given when certain types of behavior occur and not given when other types of responses are made. The probability that the response followed by reward will occur on later trials can then be made to increase. Failure of reward, or punishment, can be made to lead to a decreased probability of response ("extinction"). The studies of Herman, a computing machine, carried out by Friedberg (1958), and of the Perceptron, investigated by Rosenblatt (1958), are interesting examples of artificial learning machines. Other related possibilities are discussed in Miller, Galanter and Pribram (1960).

At a somewhat more complex level is the type of learning involved in recognizing patterns imbedded in complex stimuli. It seems a simple thing for a human to respond to a triangle as a triangle whether it is large or small, short or tall, tilted or upright, and to distinguish it clearly from a square. But to specify rigorously the criteria in such a way that a machine can learn to recognize it invariably is quite a job. And the difficulty clearly hints that there is a lot we do not understand about the phenomenon even at the human level where we take the process for granted. Selfridge (1955) and Dinneen (1955) have worked most extensively on this problem and have been able to develop methods for getting the salient features of patterns to stand out so that some uniform response is given to a particular pattern. With two techniques, one of "averaging," to get rid of random elements, and a second, of "edging," to maximize the most distinctive features, they are able to insure that a variety of different ways of writing the letter A, for example, are registered as the same letter in the computer as a basis for further processing.

The third type of learning is made possible by keeping records of success and failure attained when different methods are pursued and using these records to improve performance. Thus, in the case of the geometry computer it is possible to store theorems which have already been proved. Similar mechanisms have been incorporated into the General Problem Solver developed by Newell, Shaw and Simon (1958). It is also possible for these machines to be selective in their choice of theorems for permanent storage, rejecting those which do not seem sufficiently general to be useful later on. The most highly developed simulation of this type of learning is that incorporated in a checker-playing machine developed by Samuel (1959). His machine utilizes a type of rote learning which stores all of the checkerboard positions it encounters in play, together with the outcomes following each move. In addition this machine has some capacity to generalize on the basis of past experience and to store the generalizations themselves. With these learning mechanisms it appears possible for the computer to learn in a short period of time to play a better game of checkers than can be played by the person who wrote the program.

Many of the formulations of learning are made without any special assumptions that learning processes are consistent with known neurophysiological mechanisms. A number of students are attempting to close this gap by simulation studies of the way in which nerve networks become organized into systems and are then modified through use. There is quite extensive investigation along these lines, some of it instigated by the speculations of Hebb about the nature of nervous organization. Suffice it to say that a number of researchers have been able to program computers to simulate the changing of neural organization patterns as a result of repeated stimulation of nerve fibers and further work of a similar type is in progress (cf. Clark and Farley, 1955, and Rochester, Holland, Haibt and Duda, 1956).

In the work in our laboratory the emphasis is on understanding and simulating the processes involved in acquiring complex concepts through experience (Hovland and Hunt, 1960). The learner acquires a particular concept when he is told which of a series of specific instances presented to him belong in the concept class and which do not. This is similar to the way in which a child learns the concept of "animate" through some experiences in which parents and teachers label a given stimulus as "animate" and others in which they label it as "inanimate" (Hovland, 1952).

Our type of problem is illustrated by a situation in which there are a large number of slides of cancer cells, some of which are known to be malignant and others nonmalignant. The task of the individual (or the machine) is one of inducing the base of difference between the two types and subsequently labeling correctly new slides previously unidentified. Medical pathologists have just such a task and have achieved considerable success, although not 100 per cent accuracy, in making such distinctions. It is of interest in passing that there is a machine available which can make such a distinction on the basis of slides presented to it, but here the combination of characteristics (the "concept") was formulated by the scientist who developed the instrument (Tolles and Bostrom, 1956). The machine's task is to see whether the new specimen conforms to certain specifications, that is, whether on the basis of density and structure the cell belongs in the "malignant" or "normal" category. Thus it has the "concept" built into it, obviating the need to start from the beginning in order to induce it.

The input to the type of concept learning in which we are interested is a series of pictures, say flower designs (Hovland, 1953), some of which are labeled "positive" instances (examples of the concept) and some "negative" instances (examples of what the concept *is not*). The characteristics of the instances are represented as symbols for processing by the machine. It is hoped later to have this transformation automatic through the use of techniques developed at the Bell Telephone Laboratories which employ a television camera to convert this visual representation into electrical impulses as input to the computer. Thus the picture would become converted into one set of symbols representing the characteristics which constitute the instances of the concept (like A1B2C1D1E2F1G1H2), while another string of symbols will represent instances of what the concept *is not* (like A2B1C1D2E1F1G1H2).

Potentially, a machine can then consider combinations of all of these characteristics as possible ways of categorizing and distinguishing between the class of "A" and of "not A." Typically, human learners only attend to part of the potential set of characteristics because of perceptual limitations. We have devoted considerable research effort toward determining just how attention and perception vary during the course of learning. We have incorporated in the machine simulation a selective scanning of possible aspects of the complex stimuli with provision for the fact that some individuals see only some of the characteristics while other individuals pay attention to different aspects.

Human subjects, at least at the adult level, operate on material of this type by developing strategies involving some generalization as to what concepts are like. Some details of these strategies have been investigated by Bruner, Goodnow, and Austin (1956). The strategies may be different for different types of concepts. Logicians describe some concepts as being of the *conjunctive* type, where all the members of the class share certain common characteristics. For example, rubies share the characteristics of hardness, translucence, and redness. A second type of concept is called *disjunctive,* in which possession of either one characteristic or possession of a different characteristic makes the instance subsumable under the general class. This is illustrated by the concept of "strike" in American baseball which is either a pitched ball across the plate and between the batter's knees and shoulders *or,* alternatively, any pitch at which the batter strikes but fails to send into the field. A third type of concept is *relational,* where the instances of the concept share no common fixed characteristics but do have certain relationships in common. A sample would be the concept of "isosceles triangles." All instances of this concept involve triangles with two equal sides. But any fixed characteristics, such as lengths of the equal sides, lengths of the third side, or sizes of angles, are not an adequate basis for inclusion or exclusion in the concept class.

In preparation for later simulation, we have carried out extensive experimentation to determine the order in which these various types of concepts are considered by human learners. We find that for our type of stimulus materials, conjunctive and relational concepts are considered much more commonly than disjunctive ones (Hunt and

Hovland, 1960). So our present machine will have built into it a hierarchy of responses in which the first attempts to organize the material will be in terms of shared characteristics—conjunctive type concepts. Alternatively the machine will consider concepts which are based on relationships between the stimuli. Only when these have been extensively and unsuccessfully explored will the machine try disjunctive concept patterns.

At present, then, we have the program for a machine which is able to receive drawings having a number of different dimensions. It is then able to try a number of possible ways of organizing into a concept the prior information it has received regarding confirming and nonconfirming instances. First it considers possibilities of concepts which have various combinations of features. When none of these suffice, it considers relational concepts. When these are not successful, it considers various disjunctive concepts where one set of features or another alternative set define the concept. When a solution is reached the description of what constitutes a concept is printed out on tape and subsequent unlabeled instances are classified A's or non-A's. A scanning device is built into the machine to take into account only certain of the characteristics available for consideration. The present machine remembers all that has been presented to it. We are currently considering various devices to simulate the gradual loss of information, or forgetting, which is all too human a characteristic. Our experimental studies have indicated the over-all mathematical form which the loss should take, but there are alternative means of producing such a loss (Cahill and Hovland, 1960). Each alternative represents a different theory of the way in which forgetting occurs and investigation of the different theories is of fundamental importance. Simulation again provides a powerful tool for specifying the operation of the process of forgetting.

A high proportion of our research effort goes into new experimentation with human learners to determine their methods of handling various aspects of the problem, as compared to other efforts which stress programing the actual simulation. It is expected that this type of imbalance in effort will continue, but we are perennially hopeful that as more and more information becomes available an increasing amount of our effort will go into the simulation itself.

Work has now progressed to the point where I think we can see more clearly both the opportunities provided by these methods and some of the difficulties involved. I hope that the foregoing discussion has suggested some of the advantages of these new techniques. Let me briefly summarize the potentialities. First, simulation methods have a tremendous role in sharpening our formulations concerning mental processes and phenomena. It is one thing to say, as earlier students have said, that problem solving involves a number of different stages, for example, those of preparation, incubation, illumination, and verification, and quite another thing for one to specify exactly what is involved in each stage. The pioneering studies by Newell, Shaw and Simon (1958) on the General Problem Solver indicate the great forward strides which result from specifying the nature of these processes in such complete detail that a computer is able to solve problems by following the sequence of steps programed into the machine.

Closely related is the second advantage of the computer, the emphasis which it places on developing theories that have both descriptive and predictive power. Many of the theories which exist in psychology and sociology are so general and vague that they have little real predictive power. The program written for the computer to describe a particular process constitutes a theory which, if successful in carrying out the process in the same way as the human, is highly efficient in predicting the effects of changes in conditions and in specifying what other individuals will do under particular conditions.

Lastly, the simulation of human responses has the same overwhelming advantages for our understanding of behavioral phenomena as similar methods in other sciences. For example, the use of the wind tunnel represents a complex set of interacting conditions in actuality which could not be duplicated and whose effects could not be predicted from theory alone. Analogously in the present case, for single factors one can analyze effects without simulation, but when one seeks to understand the combined action of a number of factors interacting in complex ways, no satisfactory way of predicting the exact outcome may be possible. Those working on the geometry simulator, the General Problem Solver, and the chess and checker-playing machines, all testify to the fact that many of the moves made by the computer greatly surprised their inventors.

I hope that my remarks on the importance of simulation methods do not give rise to the feeling that these methods automatically lead to quick success in areas which have been investigated for decades using other techniques. Two examples of the difficulties confronting us may be mentioned. The first is the complexity of the process to be simulated. At present we consider ourselves fortunate if we can simulate on a machine the typical performance of a single individual in solving a particular problem. This is indeed a great step forward. But for simulation to be maximally effective we would like to be able to predict machine solutions which simulate not only a single individual under some specified condition, but also the effects for different individuals under different environmental conditions, and after various amounts of experience. To date, most simulation has been of the performance of one individual, either real or an imaginary average individual. It may prove to be extremely difficult to carry out the next step, that of specifying which characteristics must be known about each individual to be able to simulate the way he varies from the typical pattern. In addition, the effects of environmental variables, such as the effects of drugs on performance, or of pressure to complete a task, should then be simulated. Finally, the effects of experience should be specified, so that the way in which a problem is attacked is appropriately changed as a result of the machine's ability to learn. This leaves for the future such a complex problem as analysis of the interactions between type of individual and amount of learning under different environmental conditions. It is apparent that a long and difficult road lies ahead before we can accomplish successful simulation of a single type of task which has all of these variables programed. But when they can be successfully specified we will know a great deal about the problem. Most research generalizations in the social sciences are only true for a group of people, not for each individual. Computer methodology may make possible a broadening of our understanding of behavior by emphasizing the simulation of single individuals and then studying variations between them. The integration of these complementary approaches in new computer work will help us to reduce the gap between group averages and individual processes.

A second example of the difficulties of machine simulation is attributable to the nature of the process with which we are concerned. Simulation methods have most successfully been employed where it is possible to define the final performance of a task as an outcome of a succession of single steps. Thus where the mental process involves steps in a sequence one can synthesize the process by having the computing machine work first on stage one, then stage two, etc. Much more difficult are those processes where a number of stages are going on simultaneously, in parallel fashion. It certainly appears that much of our perceptual and thought process operates in this way. Under these conditions it is much more difficult to untangle the processes at work prior to simulation. In addition, present machines are not as suitable for these purposes as they are for sequential operation. New and radically different machines may ultimately be required to cope with this problem. Most of our present work is being carried out with computers which were built for quite other purposes namely high speed arithmetical computation. It would be possible to design machines more closely simulating thought processes and more flexible in their operation, but they would be expensive to construct and would not have the large number of potential purchasers who ordinarily help defray the costs of development.

Despite the difficulties mentioned, work on simulation of complex psychological processes is yielding results of increasing importance. Processes which were thought to be understood turn out to require much more explicit statement. But along with the increased explicitness comes new understanding and precision. At present most computer programs grapple with only one phase of complex processes, but we are beginning to see common features in a number of different programs, permitting the construction of comprehensive programs from simpler subprograms. Work on simulation has also had a stimulating effect on research on the higher thought processes themselves. Attempts to program computers have repeatedly revealed that we lacked much information as to how humans carry out seemingly simple thought operations. This has led to the return of workers to the laboratory which in turn has further enriched our knowledge of the human thought process.

Let not this enthusiastic report on the scientific potentialities of simulation research arouse anxieties of the sort raised by Norbert Wiener (1960) and other writers that machines will take over our civilization and supplant man in the near future. Rather, I think, there is great hope that detailed knowledge of how humans learn, think, and organize will redound to human welfare in removing much of the mystery which surrounds these processes and in leading to better understanding of the limitations of current ways of solving problems. It may, of course, become possible for us to then build machines which will work out solutions to many problems which we now consider distinctively human and to do so in a manner surpassing present human performance. But that this will lead to the machine becoming master and the designer, slave, seems to me most unlikely. Rather it will free man for novel creative tasks which are progressively beyond the capability of machines designed by man.

references

Bruner, J. S., Jacqueline J. Goodnow, and G. A. Austin, *A Study of Thinking*. New York: John Wiley & Sons, 1956.

Cahill, H., and C. I. Hovland, "The Role of Memory in the Acquisition of Concepts," *J. Exper. Psychol.*, 1960, 59, 137-144.

Clark, W. A., and B. G. Farley, "Generalization of Pattern Recognition in a Self-Organizing System," in *Proceedings of the Western Joint Computer Conference*. Institute of Radio Engineers, 1955. Pp. 86-91.

Dinneen, G. P., "Programming Pattern Recognition," in *Proceedings of the Joint Western Computer Conference*. Institute of Radio Engineers, 1955. Pp. 94-100.

Friedberg, R. M., "A learning machine, Part I," *IBM J. Res. Develpm.*, 1958, 2, 2-13. (Cf. also 1959, 3, 282-287.)

Gelernter, H. L., and N. Rochester, "Intelligent Behavior in Problem-Solving Machines," *IBM J. Res. Develpm.*, 1958, 2, 336-345.

Hovland, C. I., "A 'Communication Analysis' of Concept Learning," *Psychol. Rev.*, 1952, 59, 461-472.

————, "A Set of Flower Designs for Concept Learning Experiments," *Amer. J. Psychol.*, 1953, 66, 140-142.

————, and E. B. Hunt, "Computer Simulation of Concept Attainment," *Behav. Sci.*, 1960, 5, 265-267.

Hunt, E. B., and C. I. Hovland, "Order of Consideration of Different Types of Concepts," *J. Exper. Psychol.*, 1960, 59, 220-225.

Miller, G. A., E. Galanter, and K. H. Pribram, *Plans and the structure of behavior*. New York: Holt, Rinehart & Winston, 1960.

Newell, A., J. C. Shaw, and H. A. Simon, "Elements of a Theory of Human Problem Solving," *Psychol. Rev.*, 1958, 65, 151-166.

Rochester, N., J. H. Holland, L. H. Haibt, and W. L. Duda, "Tests on a Cell Assembly Theory of the Action of the Brain, Using a Large Digital Computer," *Trans. Info. Theory*, 1956, IT-2(3), 80-93.

Rosenblatt, F., "The Perceptron: A Probalistic Model for Information Storage and Organization in the Brain," *Psychol. Rev.*, 1958, 65, 368-408.

Samuel, A. L., "Some Studies in Machine Learning Using the Game of Checkers," *IBM J. Res. Develpm.*, 1959, 3, 211-229.

Selfridge, O. G., "Pattern recognition and modern computers," in *Proceedings of the Western Computer Conference*. Institute of Radio Engineers, 1955. Pp. 91-93.

Tolles, W. E., and R. C. Bostrom, "Automatic Screening of Cytological Smears for Cancer: The Instrumentation," *Annals N.Y. Acad. Sci.*, 1956, 63, 1211-1218.

Wiener, N., "Some Moral and Technical Consequences of Automation," *Science*, 1960, 131, 1355-1358.

3. some considerations in the design and use of dynamic flight simulators

JACK A. ADAMS

INTRODUCTION

definition

Most commonly, the term "flight simulator"[1] refers to a complex electronic device designed to reproduce with considerable fidelity for one or more aircrew stations the location and physical features of controls and instruments, the aerodynamic response of instruments and controls under various conditions of flight and operator response, switches, warning lights, radio and navigational aids, and sometimes auditory stimuli. If a combat aircraft is simulated, there usually will be armament controls, radar controls and displays (if required), and target stimuli for combat problems. Typically, flight simulators are instrument and procedures trainers which do not reproduce special stimuli, such as external visual reference cues, G-forces, or changes in bodily orientation when the simulated aircraft attitude is changed. With the exception of G-forces, one or more of these special cue classes has been reproduced in certain simulators but, in general, they are omitted from the major flight simulators in use today, often

---

[1] To limit ramifications of the training devices issue, this report will be restricted to discussion of closed-loop dynamic simulators. It will not be concerned with open-loop training devices such as functional mockups, films, or charts.

Reprinted in part from Jack A. Adams, "Some Considerations in the Design and Use of Flight Simulators," (Lackland Air Force Base, Texas: Air Force Personnel and Training Research Center, April 1957). (Research Report AFPTRC-TN-57-51, ASTIA Document No. 126382.)

because they present forbidding technical problems. State-of-the-art engineering advances are rapidly overcoming this barrier to high-fidelity simulation, and consequently there is a growing tendency to include these special stimulus classes, particularly the external visual environment.

Simulators can be arbitrarily divided into whole-task and part-task simulators. A whole-task simulator will be far more elaborate, reproducing problems of mission difficulty and complexity. In a part-task simulator only a certain difficult and critical subtask from the total job-complex is reproduced. One of the purposes of this report will be to examine simulator-complexity issues and to discuss special problems inherent in the design and use of part-task and whole-task simulators.

simulator rationale

Flight simulators have gained wide acceptance throughout the Air Force and are now an integral part of many flight training programs. Their acceptance is evidenced by the general plan for flight-simulator design and development to proceed parallel with the parent aircraft in a substantial percentage of procurement programs. Acceptance is not complete throughout the Air Force, but there seems to be a growing confidence in the value of flight simulators. In some cases the complexity of these devices, their high initial cost, and the requirements for maintenance crews, housing, and instructor personnel raise questions of economy. Yet, it has been well established that simulators can be operated for a fraction of the cost of operating the parent aircraft. Even if this cost differential were absent, the use of simulators could be well justified on the grounds that personnel can be effectively trained for situations which are prohibitively complex and expensive for routine air training and those that might be impossible to establish in the air for safety reasons.

The use of simulators for training to cope with situations which are impossible to establish in the air is not always fully appreciated. Certain aircraft emergencies are the best illustration of this class of problems. For example, single-engine jet aircraft, such as the T-33, may have an engine flameout which requires the pilot to execute an air start. Response precision and speed may be demanded if the flameout occurs at a dangerously low altitude. Standard emergency-procedure training in multi-engine aircraft calls for the deliberate failing of an engine so that the pilot can practice his air-start procedures;

but intentional flameout with single-engine jet aircraft is discouraged because of the small probability that the start will fail for equipment or pilot reasons. The absence of air-training possibilities dramatizes the importance of flight simulators where flameout cues can be presented and appropriate responses can be practiced for the acquisition and maintenance of proficiency. Certain emergencies may occur only once in a pilot's flying career, but when they occur the pilot must act with accuracy and speed if he is to complete the mission or, indeed, survive. A flight simulator appears to be one of the best ways to provide repeated and safe practice in these critical emergency procedures.

The foregoing cursory discussion of flight simulators should not be allowed to overshadow the more commonplace but important uses in transition training for new types of aircraft. A dynamic flight simulator is very valuable in familiarizing a pilot with the operating procedures and characteristics of an aircraft to which he is newly assigned. With bomber and cargo aircraft and with two-place trainer versions of single-place aircraft, some of this transition training can take place in the air with an instructor pilot. Even in these instances, however, flight simulators have a worthy role because of their low operating cost in comparison with the cost of operating modern aircraft, their independence of weather, and their suitability for teaching procedures which are impossible to teach in the air. But, when no two-place trainer version of a single-place aircraft has been built, simulators can play an even more fundamental role. Without a flight simulator the pilot transitioning to such a single-place aircraft must rely on classroom lectures and cockpit familiarization in a parked aircraft to acquire knowledge for his first solo flight. Undoubtedly many pilot responses can be acquired through the media of static classroom or cockpit displays; and this is given appropriate recognition in most flying training curricula by having extensive academic phases. However, the static approach probably has limited usefulness, particularly for continuous or procedural (discrete) responses which must be associated with one or more dynamic stimulus sources (instrument flying, radar-display interpretations, etc.). A simulator is a valuable adjunct for training in these stimulus-response classes.

A simulator reproducing the aerodynamic response of an aircraft with good fidelity is valuable for teaching new, continuous psychomotor skills required by the aircraft. If, for example, an aircraft has certain instabilities as it approaches Mach 1 and a tendency for the left wing to tuck under, prior acquaintance with these flight characteristics in the simulator can prevent slipping into dangerous attitudes at high speeds as a result of unfamiliarity with the aircraft's peculiarities. Simulator training can reduce a pilot's trial-and-error responses on his initial flights and can minimize hazards that might arise from self-generated exploratory behavior aimed toward acquiring adequate response modes.

Another problem is that aspects of a pilot's prior flying experience can transfer negatively to a new aircraft. There are numerous recorded accidents where negative transfer was the basis of death-producing errors. Intellectualizing a negative transfer problem in the classroom possibly may reduce errors, but most learning psychologists probably would agree that a flight simulator permitting actual practice of the new response to highly similar stimuli would be most effective in extinguishing the old, inappropriate response and establishing the new. One of the newest jet aircraft contains an excellent example of a negative transfer paradigm and illustrates the type of difficulty which could be minimized with adequate simulator training. The problem arises when this aircraft, either at subsonic or supersonic speeds, sometimes undergoes a longitudinal pitch-up. The normal technique to recover from the pitch-up condition is to apply nose-down stick. Sometimes, however, the aircraft will start to roll off during recovery, and the correction at this point is to move the stick *in the direction of the roll-off*. This response to correct the roll-off condition is precisely contrary to that for most other aircraft which require stick movement *in the direction opposite to the roll-off*. A flight simulator for this aircraft can save millions of dollars in equipment and many lives by permitting thorough training in such new response requirements.

The foregoing discussion broadly sketches the training importance of simulators in the modern Air Force. Their proved training value has secured their position in training programs, and the trend is clearly toward more extensive and elaborate uses of them. In addition to fulfilling training needs, flight simulators are assuming an increasingly important role in aircrew proficiency measurement. As the mission environment within which the aircrew must operate becomes increasingly elaborate and inaccessible, and as armament becomes increasingly complex and expensive, the feasibility of adequate on-the-job proficiency indexes steadily diminishes. The near impossibility of collecting aircrew performance measures within the mission context is a matter of serious consequence for commanders who must have knowledge of the combat effectiveness of their forces. Inability to get airborne proficiency measures with modern weapon systems in their combat environment leaves the simulated situation as perhaps the only context where measurement can take place.

With all these various demands on simulators as training and proficiency-measuring instruments, it is not surprising that some doubt and controversy exist on the best approach to their design and use. It is the purpose of this report to examine the rational grounds and empirical evidence relevant to some of these issues.

WHOLE-TASK SIMULATORS

Whole-task simulation is defined as a deliberate effort to achieve extensive simulation of equipment characteristics and in-flight mission factors. It should be understood at the outset that the expression "whole-task simulator" is a term of convenience. Obviously, no simulator can accurately reproduce the stimulus-response requirements of an aircraft and its operating environment in their entirety. Yet, some simulators approximate this to a far greater extent than others by including enough elements for mission exercises. These will be designated whole-task simulators.

The F-86D flight trainer is an example of a modern electronic whole-task simulator. The F-86D simulator is used primarily for checkout and transition training, although this should not be taken to imply that it is a simple familiarization device. Actually, it is one of the more sophisticated flight trainers in use. There is good duplication of the aircraft cockpit layout. The simulator possesses a high degree of capability in radar simulation and in the presentation of intercept problems, emergency situations, navigation and radio aids training, ground-controlled approach (GCA), and instrument low-approach system (ILAS) training. As an informative exercise it might be profitable to examine the salient features of the F-86D simulator in relation to some of the criteria which have been discussed [in a passage deleted above].

First, does it qualify as a whole-task simulator suitable for comprehensive combat mission exercises? When the nature of likely air defense combat missions for the F-86D is examined, the answer to this question is in the negative. A realistic analysis of these expected missions indicates that the F-86D simulator presents a grossly oversimplified mission problem. It is common knowledge that enemy bombers can be expected to be high-altitude, high-speed jets of the 600-knot class, may fly in formation, and can have the capability for such anti-interceptor actions as chaff drops and ECM [electronic countermeasures]. By contrast, the F-86D simulator can simulate an intercept problem with just one target, and this target is capable of only 500-knot groundspeed. Some ECM simulation is present, but there is no chaff simulation whatsoever (14).[2] Added to the inadequacy of special effects which emanate from targets, there is absence of atmosphere and weather effects on the radar display which importantly influence the difficulty of target detection and acquisition. Sketchy simulation of ground-return phenomena is a factor which limits mission training in low-altitude intercepts and navigation with the ground map radar mode.

Second, does the F-86D simulator provide a source of difficult mission exercises to challenge highly experienced pilots? The foregoing paragraph gives a straightforward answer by indicating that the simple intercept situations are satisfactory only for teaching task rudiments. Inability to create combat problems of realistic difficulty seriously restricts use of the simulator for advanced training.

Third, does the F-86D simulator permit good training in the critical emergency-procedures area, particularly those which cannot be practiced in the air? In training, concern is not only with the detection of emergency conditions, but also with the correct diagnosis of emergencies and whether some probability of mission completion remains or whether the mission should be aborted. In some cases, emergencies can be circumvented by pilot action, and it is important that a pilot quickly identify such emergencies and be well trained in the required responses. In general, the F-86D simulator is poor in producing the cues associated with emergencies and in reflecting a meaningful system reaction to pilot responses. In an unreported analysis of F-86D accidents, carried out by E. R. Jones and C. A. Garrett, the study of 301 cues associated with 215 F-86D accidents revealed that 72 could be adequately reproduced in the F-86D simulator, 72 could be reproduced with only partial adequacy, and 157 could not be simulated at

---

[2] It should be noted that the F-86D simulator data cited from Jones and Garrett (14) can be considered unclassified, even though their report is classified. Originally, the report was classified because of certain references to classified characteristics of the E-4 fire control system. Later discussion in this report of other F-86D simulator research (2, 3) also represents unclassified findings from reports classified for the same reason.

all.[3] In an earlier study of 1608 reported malfunctions in the E-4 fire control system and how well these are presented in the F-86D simulator, Jones and Garrett (14) found that the emergencies which could be simulated almost never occurred in flight. The simulated fire-control-system emergencies actually account for only 7 per cent of the actual difficulties while none of the cues associated with major and/or frequent emergencies could be presented.[4]

Generally, the F-86D simulator lacks the capability for full-scale mission training and for presenting difficult, advanced problems capable of challenging highly experienced pilots. Despite its inadequacies, it is an important and useful transition trainer for F-86D student pilots. Nevertheless, if radar interceptor trainers are to have a role in advanced training and have use beyond the transition phase, their design concept will have to be changed to yield simulators far more elaborate than the present one for the F-86D.

PART-TASK SIMULATORS

A part-task simulator is defined as a training device for only a critical and difficult portion of the flying task. Although any simulator is a part-task simulator in the sense that it does not reproduce the entire in-flight job, the definition is nevertheless defensible because of the deliberate concentration on one aspect of the over-all job, with no attempt to simulate the long sequence of events encountered on a mission. A part-task simulator generally is based on a difficult subtask of the mission judged to be critical to success and deserving of special, intensive practice. Because of the concentration on a specific subtask only, it can be expected that a part-task simulator will be technically less complicated and less expensive, easier to maintain, and will require less specialized instructors. Part-task simulators can be used in aspects of training for aircraft for which no whole-task simulator is available; they can be used to provide formal supplementary training in instances where neither whole-task simulator nor aircraft time is

---

[3] These data are reproduced by permission of the authors.

[4] Data collected by the American Institute for Research revealed similar inadequacies in the B-47 simulator. Of 439 reports of hazardous incidents in the B-47, one-third could not be duplicated in the simulator. In classifying the 439 incidents into 20 emergency types, 13 of the types could not be reproduced. (R. B. Miller, R. C. Craig, and G. R. Purifoy, Jr., Unpublished report: Training for emergency procedures: I. Preliminary report on techniques and recommendations for B-47 training, January 1956.)

adequate for the acquisition of proficiency in an important subtask or they can be used for informal training. This latter use suggests a self-motivating device which could be installed in lounges, ready rooms, or Base Operations, and would have "pinball machine" qualities to elicit voluntary practice. No important field tests of self-trainers have been made.

A good example of a part-task simulator for training in an operational Air Force task is the Radar Navigation Trainer developed by Searle and Murray (23). Radar motion pictures are the essential component of the trainer. A number of two-hour navigational missions were photographed, edited, and organized into a graded-difficulty series. . . . The authors express their design philosophy by stating: "The trainer is intended to provide each student with a means of acquiring skill in interpreting typical scope returns, obtaining fixes, determining wind, plotting course, and maintaining the navigational log as he would in actual flight with the APQ-13 radar equipment" (23, p. 1).

They further note that the trainer singles out only specific skills for training: ". . . no attempt is made to emphasize procedural skills in operation of the APQ-13 radar. Rather, the experimental course and the trainer have been designed to teach basic phases of radar navigation in preparation for training on the more advanced types of radar. Emphasis is placed upon realism in simulating the radar scope appearance of terrain features and upon the student's use of these returns, in conjunction with aerial charts, to acquire skill in aerial navigation" (23).

A second example is the C-11C jet instrument trainer in common use. This is a generalized trainer which does not have the flight characteristics or the cockpit layout of any particular jet aircraft. It has flight controls, basic flight instruments, and navigational aids, such as air direction finder, VHF omnidirectional range, and GCA. The instructor can establish various instrument flying problems, simulate radar control and GCA approaches, and can set in the location and characteristics of several range stations for navigation problems. A trainer of this type is consistent with the definition of part-task simulators in that it is an intentional abstraction of the instrument flying and navigation problems from the total flying complex. By providing familiarization and learning of fundamental principles and techniques, it can function (a) to reduce the number of dual instructor-student flights, which is an important economy when the cost of operating jet aircraft is considered, and (*b*) to provide more effective use of the actual flights that are made.

A third example of a part-task simulator is the MF-1(T-33A) Cockpit Procedures Trainer[5] which permits training and evaluation in an extensive range of normal and emergency procedures for the T-33A jet aircraft. The student pilot sits in a cockpit which is a good replica of the T-33A aircraft cockpit. All engine indicators and switches are active, as are other controls such as the throttle and landing gear lever. Some, but not all, of the flight instruments are active. The control column and rudder are included, but movement of them makes no input. If, for example, the student pilot had a simulated flameout at 40,000 ft. and wished to descend to 20,000 ft. before attempting an air start, he would not be able to make the altitude change himself. Instead, he would have to signal the instructor who would introduce the desired instrument changes for him. The absence of aerodynamic simulation with a focus solely on procedures serves to simplify greatly the equipment and, by this conscious concentration on the procedural aspects of the T-33A jet flying, well qualifies the trainer as a good example of a part-task simulator.

some design problems

Since a part-task simulator is a deliberate abstraction from a task complex, the designer must always face the persisting issue of "how much to simulate." The first requirement would seem to be for a job analysis which gives a detailed, time-based description of stimulus-response relationships. If the analysis reveals that the subtask activity concerned interacts or is time-shared with responses to a great many other task elements, and these elements are important for successful outcome, then it might be wise to forego a part-task simulator and conduct the training with a whole-task simulator where all task elements are present. But if certain subtask elements are subsidiary, with only secondary interactions and timesharing, then one might judge that an effective part-task simulator could be built with these peripheral subtask elements deleted.

The Radar Navigation Trainer (23) has radar motion pictures as its prime component, and was intended to provide a means of acquiring skill in interpreting typical scope returns, obtaining fixes, determining wind, plotting course, and maintaining the navigational log as

---

[5] Training Analysis and Development Division. Evaluation of the Stanley T-33A (MF-1) cockpit procedures trainer, July 1955.

would be done in actual flight with the AN/APQ-13 radar equipment. The only controls available to the trainee were a bearing-marker control knob, a range-spiral control knob, and remote-control switches for starting, stopping, or reversing the projector. A watch face, photographed simultaneously with the radar display, provided a continuous index of time lapsed during flight. The trainer included no subtask elements relevant to radar-set manipulation skills such as turning on, tuning, and adjusting the set.

An experimental study was conducted on teaching radarscope interpretation with motion pictures and amounted to a validation of the Radar Navigation Trainer (17). In the experiment, student Aircraft Observers either had all air missions (normal curriculum), half air and half motion-picture training with the Radar Navigation Trainer, or all motion-picture training. The criteria for the study were performance measures on a series of tests administered during a subsequent advanced course at Mather Air Force Base. One item of concern to the investigators was whether the absence of training in radar-set manipulation and adjustment for the film-trained students would subsequently handicap them. Evaluation of possible deficiencies was made in structured interviews and in a final course examination. The interviews with the film-trained group revealed that they felt their radar-set manipulation skills may have suffered but that this short-coming was shortlived and easily overcome in one or two air missions. The final course examination revealed no significant differences between the all air-trained group and the all film-trained group. Thus, it would appear that the designers of the Radar Navigation Trainer exercised good judgment in omitting or deemphasizing radar-set manipulation skills. Responses to those particular subtask elements obviously were easy enough to be learned within one or two sessions on the actual radar set. Without these elements the devise was greatly simplified and practice could be concentrated on task elements most fundamental to navigation problems.

FIDELITY OF SIMULATION AND TRANSFER OF TRAINING

The previous discussions have stressed the importance of determining and including appropriate classes of task elements and dimensions in whole- and part-task simulators. . . . The discussion up to now has avoided the issue of fidelity of simulation, i.e., how accurately any particular simulated task element, interaction, or situation should reproduce that of the actual operational task. For example, how closely should the "feel" of the aircraft controls in the simulator under various conditions of simulated flight resemble those of the actual aircraft under comparable circumstances? Of what importance in the simulator is fidelity of radar displays, flight characteristics of the aircraft, control-display relations, and random factors such as electronic noise which function to randomly disturb instrument readings or aspects of radar displays? Should G- forces be included? If these task elements are simulated with less than perfect fidelity, what will be the effect on transfer of training? These are among the many vexing problems that repeatedly confront simulator designers and investigators in applied human learning.

response precision

One important area for simulator design concerns how precisely control movement to a particular stimulus input should reproduce that required of the actual airborne task. For example, in executing corrections to maintain a specified aircraft on a heading, how necessary is it for the extent and pattern of control-stick movements to be exactly duplicated in the simulator? Should the radar handcontrol in an all-weather interceptor flight simulator have the same precision of manipulative movement as in the aircraft? Is it necessary that the throttle movement for a given change in revolutions per minute be precisely simulated? More generally, what are the consequences for transfer of training if the simulated control movement is more gross and imprecise than that required in the aircraft? Or, conversely, what will happen if the simulated movement is too precise and overly exacting in its response demands? These are representative questions and are among the many of this type that arise in flight simulator design. Several transfer of training experiments bear on this problem.

Using the Two-Hand Coordination Test which is a pursuit tracking task, Morin (20) found that the size of the target in training had no adverse effect in the transfer trials when subjects were required to track either a more difficult smaller target or an easier larger target. Transfer was positive and essentially complete (100 per cent), indicating that the precision of response required in training was of no consequence in determining amount of transfer. A study by Green (12) employed the same task and procedures but extended Morin's work by increasing the range of target sizes. Again, transfer was positive and complete with response precision in the training trials exercising no influence on performance in the transfer trials. Gagne and Bilodeau (9) conducted similar studies with the Rudder Control Test and manipulated response precision by varying the scoring area extent. A large scoring area was similar to a large target in the Two-Hand Coordination Test in that relatively imprecise responses were required to be on target. Their findings also revealed that positive transfer was complete and independent of response precision required in prior training trials. Moreover, there was no interaction between response precision requirements and amount of practice because transfer was positive and complete regardless of stage of training. In general, then, these experiments on response precision show that high-fidelity simulation of this variable is not necessary for high positive transfer. Although more thorough investigation of response precision is certainly required, the consistent and unitary nature of the findings is gratifying.

visual stimulus noise

There are a number of factors which can randomly disturb a stimulus while a response is being made; and whether these phenomena should be simulated has been a perturbing problem.[6] An example is the random variation that sometimes occurs in the steering information presented to the pilot in E-series fire control systems. These disturbances arise from radar scintillation, maintenance factors, and the random noise inherent in any complex electronic system. The result is that the pilot must respond to steering data which are undergoing random fluctuations and which require him to integrate information over a period of time for an estimate of the "true" path to

---

[6] This discussion of stimulus noise is not meant to include the disturbance of aircraft instruments from random air-turbulence effects. Turbulence raises special problems because it disturbs the responder as well as the stimuli and, in certain instances, removes the randomness from the stimulus deflection. To illustrate, a pilot who experiences loss of support cues from a sudden downdraft has the basis for predicting that the rate-of-climb indicator will be influenced and the direction in which its needle will be deflected. In such cases the randomness of the stimulus is attenuated because the pilot is in a position to predict stimulus action. This predictive ability is not always present, particularly for small pitch and roll disturbances. Under the latter circumstances the pilot strives to maintain proper attitude, but is required to respond on an unstable platform. The effect of randomly disturbing the responder as well as the stimuli is unknown. In particular, there is no relevant data with respect to transfer of training to guide judgments on simulating turbulence effects in flight simulators. The ME-1 simulator for the T-37 jet aircraft has reasonably sophisticated turbulence simulation and could prove a useful research instrument.

be tracked. After he has responded, noise partially or completely obscures stimulus changes resulting from the response, and knowledge of results is, therefore, inadequate or absent. Present all-weather interceptor flight simulators do not have this type of visual noise, and the question arises whether transfer of simulator tracking training to the aircraft could be improved if the noise characteristics were simulated. Briggs, Fitts, and Bahrick (7) studied this problem with the Ohio State University (OSU) Pilot Training Research Simulator (13) which uses an analog computer to simulate the two-dimensional compensatory tracking task of the E-4/F-86D system. The variable manipulated was amplitude of random noise impressed on the steering dot which the subject was required to track. All groups practiced under a no-noise condition on Day 1. On Days 2, 3, and 4 the groups practiced under either no-noise, moderate-noise, high-noise, or a varied noise condition where there was practice on four different noise levels each day. Day 5 was the transfer session, and all groups practiced under the varied noise condition. The results showed that performance level on Days 2-4 was a function of noise level, but that performance on the transfer trials on Day 5 was independent of noise level in the prior training trials. Apparently visual noise in the stimulus is a potent determiner of momentary *performance* but is not relevant for *learning* the responses required for proficiency.

proprioceptive feedback

Control "feel" issues have been persisting ones, but recent research has provided considerable clarification. One of the problems is that there are four physical properties of a control which provide proprioceptive feedback: (*a*) mass, (*b*) viscosity, (*c*) elasticity, and (*d*) coulomb friction. A full understanding of the relationships between these variables and transfer of training would require a separate as well as a combined study of them. Then, knowledge of the physical characteristics of any given control would make it possible to specify the extent to which the simulated versions must duplicate the actual control. In the absence of such comprehensive and complete laboratory data, some applied research has been conducted which deals directly with the operational equipment rather than attempting to investigate transfer as a function of the four fundamental variables concerned. University of Illinois investigators (16) experimentally studied the effect of control-stick "pressure" in the Link Trainer on transfer to the T-6 aircraft. Experimental groups trained in the Link with either high-fidelity stick pressure or near-zero pressure showed no differences in the amount of transfer to the T-6 aircraft. In similar Navy Special Devices Center project (24) three groups had SNJ Operational Flight Trainer practice with either low-, standard- (presumably high-fidelity), or high-control loadings before transfer to the SNJ aircraft. Pilot performance in the aircraft displayed no differences as a function of the amount of control loadings in the trainer. . . .

Briggs, Bahrick, and Fitts (6), using the OSU Pilot Training Research Simulator, studied the effects of control amplitude (sensitivity or control-display ratio) and/or force (spring tension) on acquisition and transfer of the tracking response. They found that these task variables were determiners of performance in the training trials, but, when the experimental groups were transferred to a control condition, there were no significant differences between groups and the amount of transfer for each experimental group was nearly 100 per cent. It was concluded that force and amplitude cues influence momentary performance but have little net effect on the basic habits required for tracking proficiency. . . .

control-display relations

A number of investigations have been carried out to determine the relative effectiveness of various control-display relationships in determining operator proficiency. An example of such research is comparison of pursuit and compensatory modes of tracking. Important as these studies are for human engineering in the design of equipment, they are of relatively little consequence in simulator design where the basic form of the control-display relationship must be the same as the parent aircraft. The principal question for simulation concerns the precision and exactness with which the basic form must be reproduced. Thus, the basic form may be retained in a simulator but the control sensitivity may be altered, the direction of display change to a specified control movement may not be exactly the same, or the mathematical functions specifying the relationships between control input and display change may differ. Whatever the changes, it is necessary to accomplish an experimental program to relate each class of changes to transfer of training. . . .

Gibbs (10) employed a compensatory tracking task with a pointer stimulus and a hand wheel control to study control-display ratio, i.e., the relationship between the magnitude of control movement and display change. Two types of changes from training to transfer trials were investigated: (*a*) change in stimulus size which, in effect, quadrupled the speed and displacement of pointer error, and (*b*) change in hand wheel size which altered the speed ratio by 2 to 1. Transfer effects were large and positive, and Gibbs concluded that high positive transfer ensues over a broad range of variation in a task dimension. . . .

Rockway (22) used a two-dimensional compensatory tracking task with a stick control to study the effect of training under low and intermediate control-display ratios on transfer to a high ratio control condition—a task where a step input yields a proportionately smaller display movement than under a low-ratio condition. Rockway found that all groups displayed significant amounts of positive transfer. The groups were ranked on the first transfer trial in accordance with the similarity between training and test ratios, but the differential effect was very transitory with no significant differences between groups by the second transfer trial.

Briggs, Bahrick, and Fitts (6), using the OSU Pilot Training Research Simulator, manipulated the control-display ratio by reducing the amplitude of stick movement required to one-fourth that of a control condition. Performance in the transfer trials where practice was under the control condition revealed almost 100 per cent transfer. Further, transfer was studied as a function of amplitude and force variation where both of these factors were reduced to one-fourth the level required of the control group. Again, transfer was about 100 per cent, indicating no interaction of force and amplitude in determining transfer.

Another relevant line of research is represented by Levine (15) who studied the effects of various constants in the task's mathematical transfer function on transfer of training. He used a one-dimensional compensatory tracking task and investigated the amount of transfer of training as a function of changes in exponential delay between control input and display response. When transfer was from various short delays to a long delay, amount of positive transfer was high and about equally efficient for any of the training delays. When transfer was from various long delays to the shortest delay, amount of transfer was directly related to the similarity between the training and transfer tasks.

Briggs, Fitts, and Bahrick (8) proceeded in a vein similar to Levine's and used the OSU Pilot Training Research Simulator to study transfer of training effects resulting from simplifying the aircraft transfer function in executing bank maneuvers. The performance of an aircraft in bank maneuvers can be approximated by two analog integrators, the first integration representing rate of roll as a function of control input, and the second representing rate of change in heading as a function of bank angle. Such double integral systems are termed acceleration systems since the system output to a step input is an accelerating function. Briggs *et al.* investigated the effects of simplified single integration or velocity system training on transfer to the more complex acceleration system. The training task was identical to the transfer task except for the absence of the first integration. Experimental groups transferred to the acceleration system after various amounts of practice on the velocity system, and were compared to a control group trained on the acceleration system throughout. The results were that the initial transfer-performance level was a function of the amount of practice on the velocity system, and that the rate of acquiring the control group's level of proficiency in the acceleration system was a function of the amount of velocity system training. The authors concluded that training on the simplified system reduced the amount of time required to achieve proficiency in the criterion task. It was emphasized, however, that the need for practice in the more complex criterion task was only reduced, not eliminated.

generalizations and qualifications

In summarizing these transfer studies, it seems clear that high fidelity of simulation is not a mandatory requirement for several prominent task dimensions. With few exceptions, training on a modified or simplified task resulted in high positive or complete transfer to the criterion task. However, it is important to note that the foregoing generalizations on transfer of training stem almost entirely from tasks of a *continuous psychomotor nature* and that safe generalizations are limited to this class of activity. Any reduction in the fidelity of visual-perceptual phenomena (radar displays, etc.) or of procedural situations which predominantly require chaining of discrete responses will demand separate transfer-of-training experiments specifically treating these task aspects.

There is good reason to believe that some classes of activity may require relatively high fidelity of simulation for certain quantities if meaningful training is to be conducted. Adams, Garrett and Robertson (3) used the F-86D flight simulator to evaluate pilot ability to interpret the prevailing flight geometry from the B-scope display. They found that meaningful presentation of scope problems required accurate simulator computation and calibration of target and inter-ceptor airspeeds and headings, target angle-off, target range and clos-ing rate. If any of these values were in error, the scope presentation inaccurately represented the flight geometry established by the in-structor. The pilot's judgment would be scored on the basis of one flight situation established by the instructor while the pilot's scope display appeared to be based on another. Little learning could take place in the presence of such ambiguity. In a related study, Adams and Garrett (2) studied F-86D pilot ability in executing lead-collision course conversions. To carry out such a conversion the pilot must make the flight geometry interpretations evaluated in the earlier study and then re-position his interceptor to compensate for deviations from the desired attack position and heading. It was found that accuracy of simulator computation was necessary for interceptor turning-radius in addition to those variables listed as critical for accurate radarscope presentations. Thus, it seems evident that whenever aircrew judg-ment and action are based on *precise* values, great care should be ex-ercised in *accurately* simulating relevant variables. A number of nor-mal and emergency procedures would be covered by this principle because pilot procedural responses are sometimes made to rather defi-nite instrument values.

references

1. Adams, J. A., "Psychomotor Response Acquisition and Transfer as a Function of Control-Indicator Relationships," *J. Exp. Psychol.*, 1954, 48, 10-14.
2. ———, and C. A. Garrett, *An F-86D Simulator Investigation of Lead Collision Course Conversion Techniques* (unclassified title). Tyndall Air Force Base, Fla.: Interceptor Pilot Research Labora-tory, Air Force Personnel and Training Research Center, May 1955. (*Technical Memorandum* IPRL-TM-55-2.) (Contents CON-FIDENTIAL.)
3. ———, C. A. Garrett, and J. G. Robertson, *Measurement of F-86D Student Pilot Ability in Radar Scope Interpretation* (unclassified title). Tyndall Air Force Base, Fla.: Interceptor Pilot Research Laboratory, Air Force Personnel and Training Research Center, June 1955. (*Technical Memorandum* IPRL-TM-55-3.) (Contents CONFIDENTIAL.)
4. Baker, Katherine E., Ruth C. Wylie, and R. M. Gagne, "Transfer of Training to a Motor Skill as a Function of Variation in Rate of Response," *J. Exp. Psychol.*, 1950, 40, 721-732.
5. Briggs, G. E., and W. J. Brodgen, "The Effect of Component Prac-

tice on Performance of a Lever-Positioning Skill," *J. Exp. Psychol.*, 1954, 48, 375-380.

6. ———, H. P. Bahrick, and P. M. Fitts, *The Influence of Force and Amplitude Cues on Learning and Performance in a Complex Tracking Task.* Lackland Air Force Base, Tex.: Air Force Personnel and Training Research Center, March 1957. (*Research Report* AFPTRC-TN-57-33, ASTIA Document No. 098938.)

7. ———, P. M. Fitts, and H. P. Bahrick, *Learning and Performance in a Complex Tracking Task as a Function of Visual Noise.* Lackland Air Force Base, Tex.: Air Force Personnel and Training Research Center, June 1956. (*Research Report* AFPTRC-TN-56-67.)

8. ———, P. M. Fitts, and H. P. Bahrick, *Transfer Effects from a Single to a Double Integral Tracking System.* Lackland Air Force Base, Tex.: Air Force Personnel and Training Research Center, December 1956. (*Research Report* AFPTRC-TN-56-135, ASTIA Document No. 098912.)

9. Gagne, R. M., and E. A. Bilodeau, *The Effects of Target Size Variation on Skill Acquisition.* Lackland Air Force Base, Tex.: Air Force Personnel and Training Research Center, April 1954. (*Research Bulletin* AFPTRC-TR-54-5.)

10. Gibbs, C. B., "Transfer of Training and Skill Assumptions in Tracking Tasks," *Quart. J. Exp. Psychol.*, 1951, 3, 99-110.

11. ———, "The Continuous Regulation of Skilled Response by Kinesthetic Feedback," *Br. J. Psychol.*, 1954, 45, 24-39.

12. Green, R. F., "Transfer of Skill on a Following Tracking Task as a Function of Task Difficult (Target Size)," *J. Psychol.*, 1955, 39, 355-370.

13. Harter, G. A., and P. M. Fitts, *The Functional Simulation of Complex Systems by Means of an Analog Computer, with the F-86D, E-4 System as a Specific Example.* Parts I and II. Lackland Air Force Base, Tex.: Air Force Personnel and Training Research Center, December 1956. (*Research Report* AFPTRC-TN-56-133: Part I (unclassified), ASTIA Document No. 098909; Part II (Contents CONFIDENTIAL), ASTIA Document No. 098910.)

14. Jones, E. R., and C. A. Garrett, *Characteristics of the F-86D-19 Flight Simulator.* Part II (unclassified title). Tyndall Air Force Base, Fla.: Interceptor Pilot Research Laboratory, Air Force Personnel and Training Center, October 1954. (*Technical Memorandum* IPRL-TM-54-1.) (Contents CONFIDENTIAL.)

15. Levine, M., *Transfer of Tracking Performance as a Function of a Delay Between Control and Display.* Wright-Patterson Air Force Base, Ohio: Wright Air Development Center, November 1953. (WADC *Technical Report* 53-237.)

16. Matheny, W. G., A. C. William, Jr., Dora J. Dougherty, and S. G. Hasler, *The Effect of Varying Control Forces in the P-1 Trainer Upon Transfer to the T-6 Aircraft.* Lackland Air Force Base, Tex.: Air Force Personnel and Training Research Center, September 1953. (*Technical Report* AFPTRC-TR-53-31.)

17. McClelland, W. A., P. S. Abbott, and W. H. Stobie, *Teaching Radarscope Interpretation with Motion Pictures: I. Radar Navigation, the Ellington Study.* Lackland Air Force Base, Tex.: Air Force Personnel and Training Research Center, July 1954. (*Technical Report* AFPTRC-TR-54-25.)

18. McGeoch, J. A., and A. L. Irion, *The Psychology of Human Learning,* revised ed. New York: Longmans, Green, 1952.

19. McGuigan, F. J., and E. F. Mac Caslin, "Whole and Part Methods in Learning a Perceptual Motor Skill," *Amer. J. Psychol.,* 1955, 68, 658-661.

20. Morin, R. E., "Transfer of Training Between Motor Tasks Varying in Precision of Movement Required to Score," *Amer. Psychol.,* 1951, 6, 390 (Abstract).

21. Muckler, F. A., and W. G. Matheny, "Transfer of Training in Tracking as a Function of Control Friction," *J. Appl. Psychol.,* 1954, 38, 364-367.

22. Rockway, M. R., *The Effect of Variations in Control-Display During Training on Transfer to a "High" Ratio.* Wright-Patterson Air Force Base, Ohio: Wright Air Development Center, October 1955. (WADC *Technical Report* 55-366.)

23. Searle, L. V., and N. L. Murray, *The Radar Navigation Trainer* (unclassified title). Mather Air Force Base, Calif.: Human Resources Research Center, May 1952. (*Research Note* AO-52-5.) (Contents CONFIDENTIAL.)

24. Wilcoxon, H. C., and E. Davy, *Fidelity of Simulation in Operational Flight Trainers. Part II. The Effect of Variations in Control Loadings on the Training Value of the SNJ OFT.* Port Washington, N.Y.: Navy Special Devices Center, January 1954. (*Technical Report* 999-2-3B.)

4. simulated bureaucracies: a methodological analysis

MORRIS ZELDITCH, JR., Stanford University

WILLIAM M. EVAN, Massachusetts Institute of Technology

In sociology and social psychology the laboratory experiment has become associated almost exclusively with the investigation of small, simply-structured, face-to-face groups. It is true that Bavelas has created somewhat more complex structures;[1] Guetzkow has simulated business firms and international systems;[2] and operations research and gaming have simulated very complex and lifelike organizations,[3] although seldom for sociological purposes. But that the connection between the laboratory experiment and simplicity of social structure is largely accidental and unnecessary is not yet widely accepted among sociologists. It may be useful, therefore, to review

---

[1] A. Bavelas, "Communication patterns in task-oriented groups," *Journal of the Acoustical Society of America*, 22 (1950), 725-730.

[2] H. Guetzkow, and A. E. Bowes, "The development of organizations in a laboratory," *Management Science*, 3 (1957), 380-402; and H. Guetzkow, "A use of simulation in the study of inter-nation relations," *Behavioral Science*, 4 (1959), 183-191.

[3] Among others, see: R. Bellman, *et al.*, "On the construction of a multi-stage multi-person business game," *Operations Research* 5 (1957), 469-503; C. W. Churchman, and P. Ratoosh, "Innovation in group behavior," Working paper No. 10, Management Science Nucleus, Institute of Industrial Relations, University of California, Berkeley 1960; D. F. Clark, and R. L. Ackoff, "A report on some organizational experiments," *Operations Research*, 7 (1959), 279-293; S. Enke, "On the economic management of large organizations: a laboratory study," *Journal of Business*, 31 (1958), 280-292; R. M. Rauner, *Laboratory Evaluation of Supply and Procurement Policies*, RAND Report R-323, 1958 (Unclassified); F. M. Ricciardi, *et al.*, *Top Management Decision Simulation: The AMA Approach*, (AMA Inc., New York, 1957).

Published here for the first time with the permission of the authors.

some of the functions of laboratory simulation, the principal considerations in constructing simulates, and, in view of the usual attack on their artificiality, to point out where the dangers in simulation are and are not to be found—all in the context of a problem of sociological relevance, the creation of experimental bureaucracies. By simulation here we mean the laboratory study of structures, the properties of which have been simplified, transformed, or substituted for other properties in naturally occurring structures.[4]

FUNCTIONS OF SIMULATION

The natural world has certain disadvantages from the point of view of observation and theory construction. Certain states of great theoretical interest occur quite rarely, while other states, of little theoretical interest, occur profusely. Certain effects of great theoretical interest are obscured by other effects which are, although powerful, of little interest. And there are always more relevant variables than any observer or any theory could conceivably take into account at one time. Through simulation, such processes may be simplified, measured, and manipulated, so that rare states may be created, reasonably exact replicates ensured, necessary contrasts obtained, confounding factors randomized, extraneous disturbances eliminated, and the process observed comprehensively, precisely, and more or less at the will of the investigator.

rare states

Where a variable's natural range of variation is narrow it is difficult to investigate its effects. It will appear uncorrelated with other variables and may even seem irrelevant to a system of variables in which, in fact, it plays an important part. The same thing can be said for states that are not so much rare as costly or destructive, such

---

[4] Our discussion of simulation is severely limited, in two respects: First, to simulation for research, rather than training, despite the fact that simulation is used much more for the latter than the former; second, to simulation which is inductive, or nontautologous, rather than deductive, or tautologous. The latter programs a set of assumptions into a computer—or man and computer together—which performs a long chain of deductive operations for the investigator, yielding implications that simpler mathematics or the unaided mind could not obtain; or, quite frequently, many programs are tried, the purpose being to find that set of assumptions which best yields a known set of implications (empirical knowledge), hence increasing the power and generality of a theory.

as war, or not in the investigator's control, such as an arms race.[5] A very important example of a rare state arises when the effect of *a* on *b* is lagged, but the process is, in natural settings, usually found in an advanced stage of progress so that it is difficult to investigate how *a*'s effect on *b* comes about. This is often true of the process by which social structures are built up. To study such states simulation seems a necessary strategy.

replicates

Where relatively unique structures are investigated, or where very few of them exist, it is useful to simulate them so that many and exact replicates are provided for investigation. For example, there is only one system of international relations, and even its components are relatively few in number, complex, large, freely varying. Hence, Guetzkow[6] has found it useful, for training purposes, to simulate the foreign policy apparatus of a set of simplified nations with fixed and manipulable characteristics and processes. This simulation can produce as many replicates of an international system as costs permit.

contrasts

The classic *ex post facto* method of dealing with contamination is to hold constant the contaminating factor, *c*. But where *a* and *c,* or *b* and *c,* are highly correlated in natural settings, obtaining a sufficient number of the necessary contrasts may be costly or even impossible. In such a case it may be useful or necessary to create the required contrasts artificially. The contaminant may be a *cancelling* factor, the effects of which run counter to the effect of *a;* an *additive* factor, independent of *a* but obscuring the relative importance of *a;* an *irrelevant* factor, unrelated to *b* but highly correlated with *a* so that the package *ac* requires purification; or a *confounding* factor, spuriously generating the correlation between *a* and *b*. The first three effects may be investigated by the usual methods of field studies and surveys if appropriate contrasts are available; but sometimes, perhaps often, they are not. The effects of confounding are never entirely controlled by investigations in natural settings, since randomization is the only (relative) safeguard against the indefinitely large number of relevant factors of which we are, at any moment, quite ignorant.

---

[5] Cf. Rauner, *op. cit.,* and Enke, *op. cit.*
[6] H. Guetzkow, *op. cit.*

disturbance and complexity

The real world is intricate, entangled, continuously varying. It is virtually impossible to study all variables at once; it is equally impossible to study a small subset of them while these are continuously altered by the effects of some larger set. The subset may, in fact, appear to be entirely without regularity if the variables in the "external" set are not held constant. *Simplification* reduces the number of variables, and often their permissible values; *isolation* removes the investigated system from the effects of a varying environment. Isolation may be accomplished *ex post facto,* just as the control of other factors may be. But there is a severe limit to the number of external factors that can be so controlled and, like confounding factors, their number is indefinitely large and our own knowledge of them is limited.

observation

A simulate is usually small by comparison with the real system it represents; it can be instrumented at will; and its processes can be started, and often even stopped, at will. These properties make it readily observable. Because of them simulation is often convenient and useful even where none of the previous functions is served. Of these properties, optional starting is perhaps the most useful. Complete investigation of a response curve is facilitated if one is able to vary the initial states at will; and complete investigation of a correlation is facilitated if one is able to reverse the relations of variables at will. It is particularly an advantage where the effect in which we are interested occurs in a very brief period of time or in minute magnitudes, and repetition is consequently a great help.

STRUCTURE OF THE SIMULATE

Where some particular theory is concerned, such as organizational theory, the important decisions in constructing simulates are: (1) What properties in the theory must be incorporated in the simulate? (2) How many properties? (3) What kinds of properties?

"In utilizing the simplifications of the laboratory," Guetzkow and Bowes have cautioned, "it is important to avoid that simulation which eliminates the organizational phenomenon itself."[7] Organizational

---

[7] H. Guetzkow, and A. E. Bowes, *op. cit.,* p. 400.

phenomena may be eliminated in two opposed directions: (1) by constructing simulates of the most general social systems, of which, of course, organizations are a subclass; (2) by simulating simply-structured subunits of organizations. Parsons and Bales, in the *Working Papers,* have thought of their small groups in the former way, and of course a very large literature exists in which small groups are thought of in the latter way. Both types of investigation yield information relevant to organizational theory. But the theory of organizations appears to deal with a distinct emergent level not predictable from the properties of its subunits and more special than the general theory of social systems. Hence its simulation ought to represent at least its class-defining properties—those which distinguish organizations from other social systems. While the distinguishing criteria of organizations will be controversial until the theory is better developed, they probably include: formalization; functional differentiation; restricted chains of command and communication; and a resultant complexity of units and rank-levels.[8] It is not, we believe, required that simulation *activate* every part of this organization, so long as the parts activated have organizational properties and are seen by participants as part of an organization with such properties. This may be simulated by instructions to participants and by environmental inputs to the part being activated. Participants should at least see themselves in organizational statuses.

Simulations simplify; some, however, have many properties and some have few. A simulate that is very rich in properties is as difficult to observe, control, and analyze as the world it represents. But a simulate that is poor in properties depends, more than a rich one, upon a theory sufficiently developed to translate its results into terms relevant to an understanding of empirical reality. Even so highly developed a field as the sociology of organizations is as yet too undeveloped to justify highly simplified simulates. Hence, in the present state of theory, we require simulates close to the upper bound of richness; the upper bound is dictated by the desire to isolate and manipulate theoretically significant variables without undue complication.

Simulation usually uses at least some *real* properties, identical with those in the natural setting. Transformation and substitution also

---

[8] For an expansion of this view, see M. Zelditch and T. K. Hopkins, "Experiments with organizations," in A. Etzioni, (ed.), *Complex Organizations: A Sociological Reader* (New York: Holt, Rinehart and Winston, Inc., 1961).

yield three other kinds of properties: *iconic* properties, transformed in scale but otherwise the same as the properties they represent (for example, simulation may represent a year's time by an hour's time); *analogue* properties,[9] in which one property is substituted for another, but behaves in the same way as the property for which it substitutes (for example, a computer may represent a commodity market in a business game, but be so constructed that it obeys the same laws as a market, so far as these are now known); and *homologue* properties, in which one property is substituted for another, but the substitute bears only a surface similarity to the property which it represents (for example, this is probably true of Leavitt's simulation of "organizational histories" by the different target sequences of a number puzzle).[10]

The instructive experience of experimental geology suggests how critical is the distinction between the last two types—difficult as it is to make in practice. Geologists began simulation over sixty years ago, but at first without notable success except occasionally and accidentally. Their early simulates were miniature but morphologically exact representations of the real world. They used, for example, the same materials, shale for shale, etc. Because of their morphological exactness the forces operating in the scale model were distorted in their effects; the materials were too hard by comparison with the forces represented. It was finally discovered that by using asphalt or similar materials to represent rock better results were obtained. The viscosity of such materials more closely approximated the theoretical relationship of forces in the systems of variables simulated.[11] The properties of a simulate need not *look* like the properties they represent; what is required is that they obey the same laws. This might be called *the rule of genotypic similarity.*

But the rule of genotypic similarity, like the rule of simplification,

9 The labels "icon" and "analogue" are borrowed, although with somewhat different meanings attached to the "analogue" property, from R. L. Ackoff, "Games, decisions, and organizations," GENERAL SYSTEMS, 4 (1959), 145-150. Ackoff borrows "icon," in turn, from Peirce. Other sources in which types of simulates are discussed include: A. Chapanis, "Men, machines, and models," *American Psychologist,* 16 (1961), 113-131, and M. Shubick, *Bibliography on Simulation, Gaming, and Allied Topics,* Second Revised Ed., (New York: Operation Research and Synthesis Consulting Service, 1960). Introduction.

10 H. J. Leavitt, "Task-ordering and organizational development in the common target game," *Behavioral Science,* 5 (1960), 233-239.

11 V. V. Belousov, "Experimental Geology," *Scientific American* 204, No. 2, (1961), 97-106.

depends on a theory that informs us of how the relevant properties should behave. In the absence of theoretical justification—a condition frequent in the theory of organizations—there is little ground for distinguishing analogue from homologue properties. Hence, the most fruitful simulate at the present juncture in the development of organizational theory is probably the *heuristic* simulate, both rich in properties and made up mostly of real and iconic properties. As theory accumulates, simulates should become less rich and use more analogue properties.

SIMULATED BUREAUCRACY: AN ILLUSTRATION

In a companion paper we report the results of an experiment in which a simulated organization is used to separate the *rational* and *legal* components of Weber's ideal bureaucracy. Empirical consequences for performance, conformity, and legitimation of authority are examined in that paper. Here we consider why we chose to simulate, what properties were simulated and what properties were not, and what kinds of properties they were.[12]

> Forty-five Columbia College students were hired during their Easter vacation to code for a fictitious survey research organization called NATIONAL SOCIAL SURVEYS, INC., at the rate of $1.25 an hour. They were trained three at a time by an instructor, who was identified as project director, to code the face sheet of a questionnaire. The project director also instructed S's in the purposes and rules of the organization, emphasizing its professional character, interest in valid results, objectivity, contribution to knowledge, etc. After about half an hour of instruction, S's were taken to separate rooms—it was explained that working independently increased accuracy and efficiency—where the only other person was an observer who, if asked, said he was working on another project and knew nothing about S's project. The observer recorded non-verbal gestures and any comments made by S.
>
> S's could communicate with their supervisors by telephone only. They were given code sheets, face sheets, time sheets, code books, and general rules to follow; if they got into difficulty they were told to call their supervisors. The independent variable—we varied knowledge while holding authority of office constant—was induced through the supervisor's responses to these telephone calls. To ensure uniform administration of the experimental stimulus, the face

---

[12] For substantive details, see W. M. Evan and M. Zelditch, Jr., "A laboratory experiment on bureaucratic authority," *American Sociological Review,* 26 (1961), 883-893.

sheets contained, at fixed intervals, "trap" items for which the code book gave inadequate instruction; and through pretesting we reduced the number of other items on which calls would occur to a relatively small number.

For forty-five minutes all subjects had supervisors who were superior in technical knowledge. This increased homogeneity of subjects, gave them a baseline so that they could evaluate supervisors, and provided *before*-measures so that, through repeated measurement of the same individuals, we could guard against effects of individual variation in ability and personality. Supervisors then called *S*'s and informed them that they would be assigned to new supervisors—the old ones had to leave. Supervisors then rotated—changing telephone numbers made this simple, and no *S* called his old supervisor by mistake—and were, with respect to their new coders: (1) inferior in knowledge; (2) about equal to the coder in knowledge; or (3) superior in knowledge. In the first case the supervisor always said he did not know how to deal with the presented problem; in the second he sometimes said this, and sometimes also asked the coder what he thought should be done; in the third the supervisor always gave a reasonable response backed by technical knowledge displayed in the discussion of the problem. A messenger of the organization brought new face sheets to code at this time, again to ensure a uniform experimental stimulus, explaining that the new batch was needed more immediately. Supervisors gave not only technical commands and instructions, but also administrative commands, since these were expected to produce different results. The experiment is a randomized complete blocks design in which the second period supervisors are the blocks. *S*'s were randomly allocated to treatments and blocks. There were no block effects nor treatment x block interactions, showing that the supervisors played their roles well and equally so across all three supervisor-roles.

After a second forty-five minute period, *S*'s were interviewed by interviewers from a second fictitious organization, a management research corporation seeking to improve the operation of NATIONAL SOCIAL SURVEYS. The post-session interview asked questions designed to validate the independent variable and measure legitimacy. The experiment was then explained, and *S*'s, disturbed at finding they did not have real jobs, were referred to actual coding jobs on real projects. By running trials in tandem (instruction of new *S*'s overlapped interviewing of old *S*'s) the entire experiment was run off in three days. Interaction of *S*'s outside the experiment was virtually eliminated because for the most part they were at home for Easter and had little time to get together during this short period.[13]

---

[13] Performance was not affected by the treatments, but conformity decreased with increasing discrepancy of office and knowledge. Although all *S*'s

We decided on an experiment for several reasons. First, although we believed that office and knowledge were conceptually independent, locating a sufficient number of instances in real organizations seemed to us a costly and inefficient process.[14] Secondly, where the discrepancy was systematic, as in lay administration of professional organizations, the effects were obscured by organizational accommodations to the discrepancy, such as multiple lines of authority and distinctions between administrative and professional decisions.[15] Third, control of the large number of contaminating variables that occurred to us seemed from our own field experience hopeless; the age and ethnic backgrounds of the supervisors, their personalities, the abilities and backgrounds of subordinates, their interaction with each other, non-work related interaction of supervisors and subordinates, structure of the labor market, variations in professional orientation, career plans, etc., are only a beginning list of relevant factors. We were, at the time, ignorant of the simulations that had already been reported, mostly by operations researchers; but it seemed to us we could create our own organization, ensure exactness of replicates, better measure the process, and still produce the phenomenon in which we were interested.

The experiment we designed makes little use of transformation or substitution of properties. Scale time is equal to real time, scale wages are equal to real wages, features enforced by the nature of the experiment's façade. For the same reason substitution occurs only in the means of communication, which in such an organization would probably in a natural setting have been face to face. The experimental simulate is, however, very much simplified. The effects of age, ethnic backgrounds, and personalities of supervisors are eliminated both through randomization and the use of telephone communication. Supervisors and subordinates have no non-work interaction. Interaction of subordinates is not permitted and, through before-after

continued to regard their supervisors as legitimate, regardless of treatment, discrepancy between office and knowledge caused them to shift the bases of legitimacy from "professional" to "bureaucratic."

[14] For an example of the difficulty of locating theoretically necessary contrasts in a field study, see William M. Evan, "Some Consequences of a Discrepant Authority Relationship," *Proceedings and Summaries of the 23rd Annual Meeting, New York State Psychological Association,* (May, 1960), pp. 32-34.

[15] See, for example, M. Goss, *Physicians in Bureaucracy,* Columbia University, unpublished doctoral dissertation, 1959.

measurements, their personalities and abilities affect only the size of the error term used in the analysis of variance.

Is the simulate *over*-simplified? As far as possible we tried to reproduce many real properties of a professional bureaucracy: the organization is formal; its statuses are replaceable; it is guided by the rule of law; office and person are separated; it has a restricted chain of command and communication; subjects are "employees," rather than "subjects" and have organization rather than small group statuses; technical competence and professional training are important qualifications for office.

It is not a replica of the whole organization, since only the dyadic supervisor-coder relationship operates through most of the experiment. But through instructions, and through inputs from external structures, the subject is made to think of himself as having a status in a larger, complex organization, some of the other statuses of which he occasionally sees (messenger, project director). Simulates in which a part of the organization is activated while the remainder is created only by inputs to the activated part may be called *part replicas*.[16]

However, the simulate *is* overly simple in three important ways. First, the organization is a professional organization, but the S's are not professionals; and external professional associations, of great importance in natural settings, impinge in no way on these experimental bureaucracies. Second, because they are temporary help the S's are not oriented to a career in the organization, nor is any kind of career line simulated. Third, the time span of the organization, precisely because it is not transformed in scale, is unrealistically short. This does not affect the meaning of the situation to the S's, so much as it does the process linking office without knowledge to its consequences, for this process may very well differ as task-time increases or as the employee is given more and different tasks. The validity and generality of the experiment's results must be assessed in this light.

FUNCTIONS AND DYSFUNCTIONS OF ARTIFICIALITY

Simulation manipulates, simplifies, transforms, and substitutes other properties for the properties of the natural world: it is artificial.

---

16 Compare Zelditch and Hopkins, *op. cit.*, where experiments are classified, from the point of view of their relevance to organizational theory, into *miniature replicas, part replicas, near organizations,* and *simply-structured groups.*

This may or may not be a defect, depending on the *sense* in which it is artificial. A simulation may be artificial in the sense that:

(1) Its independent variables are given unreal values, although they are the same variables that operate in the natural world and, if left to themselves, would yield descriptively natural results. *Example:* "free communication" permitted in a bureaucratic organization.

(2) Its correlated properties, those describing the setting of the experiment, motivation of the subjects, etc., may differ from those which the simulation represents. *Example:* college students as subjects where executive board committee meetings of business corporations are represented.

(3) Its properties do not behave like real properties. *Example:* puzzles to represent the tasks of a bureaucratic organization.

That "real" variables may take on unreal values is no defect; this is precisely the purpose, or one of the purposes, of the simulation. To justify this artificiality it is perhaps necessary to believe that theory construction is an important task, because it is largely in the interests of theory that such states are created.[17] Because attention is focussed on the relations among a system of variables, more than on their actually descriptive states, effects that do not frequently occur are as illuminating as effects which do. If a variable c almost always cancels the effect of a variable a on b in the natural world, it may be of little interest so far as our descriptive knowledge of that world is concerned to discover that b is a linear increasing function of a. Only an interest in theory construction would lead to the separation of the a and c effects. Hovland, for example, has produced attitude change in the laboratory by, among other things, preventing S's from controlling their own exposure to stimuli. In natural settings very much less change occurs because exposure is optional. This limits the value of Hovland's findings from a descriptive point of view; but they are not less illuminating because of this.[18]

---

[17] This is not the same as saying, as is sometimes said, that interest is in verification as distinct from discovery and exploration. We may simulate in relatively undeveloped stages of theory in order to examine unusual conditions and their consequences, or simply to better control the conditions under which a phenomenon is observed, and our interest is nevertheless in theory construction. Proof is not the sole, nor even the most frequent function of simulation.

[18] For Hovland's discussion of this problem see: C. I. Hovland, "Reconciling conflicting results from experimental and survey studies of attitude change," *American Psychologist,* 14 (1959), 8-17.

It is Tolman who is reputed to have asked: "Are college students people?" They are, of course, very convenient and accessible subjects. They might, in this respect, be compared to the fruit-fly. The analogy bears extension. The geneticist finds the fruit-fly a strategic and convenient research subject because the relevant process is run through so rapidly, there are so many replicates, and they are so readily confined and observed. But what is so important about the fruit-fly is that its genetic process is not fundamentally different from the human genetic process. Neither its size nor its structure is correlated with the process investigated. The study of enzymes, of vertebrate anatomy, of temperature adaptations, of any one of a hundred problems easily named, requires a different experimental subject.

Of the college student too it must be asked, are the ways in which he differs from other people correlated with the effects investigated? In some cases probably not; for example, an elegant set of experiments by Siegel and Fouraker on monopolistic competition is probably little affected by the fact that subjects are students.[19] In some cases probably yes; for example, Guetzkow's simulated international diplomacy is excellent for teaching, but less adequate for experimental purposes because the college students probably differ from diplomats in ways relevant to the results desired of the simulate.[20]

It is of course not necessary to use college students. But even so, are not experimental settings intrinsically so unlike real organizations that experimental results are impossible to generalize? Experimental groups are, after all, small, *ad hoc,* transitory, and of little significance to their members, whereas organizations are in most respects the opposite. But size and duration are not really relevant; it is what they are usually supposed to correlate with that is relevant—complexity and degree of institutionalization. And these can be simulated experimentally, as, for that matter, can involvement; so that the character of the usual experimental group is no bar to experiments with organizations. The properties that cannot be much altered, size and duration, are not themselves correlated with the processes investigated; and the properties that are correlated, low institutionalization and involvement, are not at all necessary properties of experimental groups and can be altered.[21]

It is one thing to accuse simulation of creating unreal states; it is

---

[19] S. Siegel and L. E. Fouraker, *Bargaining and Group Decision Making* (New York: McGraw-Hill Book Co., 1960).

[20] H. Guetzkow, *op. cit.*

[21] This argument is expanded in Zelditch and Hopkins, *op. cit.*

quite another to accuse it of creating unreal relationships. If the former is one of the principal functions of simulation, the latter is one of its principal dangers. When artificiality is criticized, it is here that the critic is most to the point. But at the same time, this is not so much artificiality as it is simply bad simulation. No purpose of simulation dictates that it should yield unreal properties. The other side of the rule of genotypic similarity is that, however unlike the properties of the natural setting the properties of the simulate may *look,* they must *behave* in the same way or the simulation has failed in its intent. It may be permissible, even advisable, to substitute for properties of the real world other properties in the simulate; but no substitution is admissible which arbitrarily substitutes one property for another without their behavior being compared. Does this again require a developed theory? Not theory, necessarily, but rather it requires careful validation procedures. To this end, before experimenting on a simulate the investigator ought to run a sufficiently long series of uniformity trials to show that, left to itself, the simulate behaves like the process simulated at least in those ways necessary to the investigation.[22] And, obviously, in order to know how the process stimulated behaves it is necessary to conduct field research or else fall back on relevant studies of natural settings by other investigators.[23] While theory can go a long way in generalizing laboratory findings to reality, the coordination of observations of laboratory and field research is as essential for progress in organizational theory as in any other area in social science.[24]

---

[22] Validation, for example, is the principal result of work reported by Churchman and Ratoosh, *op. cit.*

[23] Of general importance for our discussions of artificiality and making the transition between the findings of laboratory and field studies, see H. W. Rieken, *et al.,* "Narrowing the Gap Between Field Studies and Laboratory Experiments in Social Psychology: A Statement of the Summer Seminar," *SSRC Items,* 8 (1954), 37-42.

[24] Cf. Leon Festinger, "Laboratory Experiments: The Role of Group Belongingness," in James Grier Miller, *Experiments in Social Process* (New York: McGraw-Hill Book Co., 1950), pp. 33-34; John R. P. French, Jr., "Field Experiments: Changing Group Productivity," in Miller, *Idem.,* pp. 90 ff.

5. analysis of social structures and simulation of social processes with electronic computers

JAMES S. COLEMAN

The problems with which sociologists have concerned themselves in recent years have tended to be "individualistic." Sociologists have studied why people buy this or that product, why they vote for a candidate, why some work harder than others, why some are more interested in education than others, why some are more delinquent or criminal than others, what people do with their leisure time.

This focus constitutes a shift away from an older tradition in sociology, a tradition of Marx, Durkheim, Toennies, all of whom were concerned with the functioning of social systems. In part, the shift away from this tradition has been merely a shift away from large-scale problems of social speculation to problems which can be studied by systematic research. But the shift has gone even further than that, for it has gone down to the level of the individual himself. I think a good part of the problem can be laid at the feet of research techniques: we interview or observe *individuals,* punch the information up on individual and separate IBM cards, and then proceed to analyze—not the social system, but the IBM cards.

Electronic computers combine, for the first time, the ability to

This is the second of two papers presented at the University of Texas Lecture Series, on the Impact of Computers on Behavioral Sciences Research, March 30 and 31, 1960. [Reprinted in part from James S. Coleman, "Analysis of Social Structures and Simulation of Social Processes With Electronic Computers," Working Paper No. 4, National Science Foundation—G945. Also reprinted from *Educational and Psychological Measurement* XXI, No. 1 (1961), 203-218, with the permission of the author and G. Frederic Kuder.]

handle these masses of quantitative data with the ability to take into account *structural connections* between various parts. The memory of a computer consists of a large array of memory cells or storage locations. The machine can compare information between two cells just as easily as it can compare information within the same cell. Consequently, we no longer have forced upon us the sharp separation between different parts of a social system. In effect, the structure of a community under study can be laid out on the memory cells of a computer—and the analysis can study, not *individuals'* responses, but the structure itself.

Now this is no simple task, because it requires a kind of analysis totally different from the quantitative analyses we are accustomed to. The dependent variable need no longer be the behavior of the individual, but can be the behavior of the system itself. It is much nearer a synthesis—much more like the anthropologists' weaving together of pieces to recreate a functioning community—than that of the survey researcher's analysis of why people change jobs.

Example—Cliques. In a study of high schools I have found the following situation: in each grade of high school, there is a "leading crowd." In the small schools (around 500 pupils) the leading crowd of boys is a single clique who name each other as friends; and the leading crowd of girls is a single clique in each grade. There are curious exceptions to this for both boys and girls: in the predominantly working-class schools, there is a bifurcation of the boys' leading cliques into two during the *senior* year—and a bifurcation of the girls' leading cliques into two in the *sophomore* year. The cause? Apparently this: in a working-class school, the boys' leading clique includes a large component of boys who will not attend college, along with some who will. Only in the senior year do the paths of these boys truly diverge—in terms of the courses they take, their out-of-school activities, and the things they talk about when they are together—so that the clique breaks up into a college-going one and a non-college-going one.

The situation is different for girls. It is during the sophomore year that the activities of the girls diverge sharply, and not on the basis of college-going vs. non-college-going. They diverge rather on the basis of dating. One segment of the leading crowd begins to date with some frequency, while another segment does not. The dating segment breaks away and constitutes a separate clique.

Two separate kinds of analysis are required to find results like this which come from the quantitative analysis of a social system as a system. First, an analysis of the structure, which separates the system into the cliques of which it consists, and relates the clique structure to membership in the "leading crowd," is needed. Second, one must have an analysis of what each of the cliques has in common, differentiating it from other cliques. Neither of these analyses can be easily carried out by conventional punched-card techniques, simply because they are both problems involving *structure*.

Example—Reference Group Phenomena. The specific problem is one which arose in the high school study mentioned above. The problem might be termed one of "reference-group behavior." I asked each boy and each girl which other boy or girl in school he would most like to be like. I wanted to know to what degree a boy's or girl's aspirations and attitudes were affected by the attributes of the person he looked up toward. That is, to what degree does the person so named *actually* serve as a point of reference for the people who named him as the person they want to be like? Or, conversely, to what degree do their attitudes cause them to shift their point of reference to someone else more consistent with these attitudes? Since a questionnaire was administered at the beginning and end of the school year, this problem could be examined by seeing changes over the given school year.

The attitude with which we were concerned is one expressed in answer to the following question:

If you could be remembered in high school in any of these ways, which would it be?

> Brilliant student
> Athletic Star
> Most popular

The corresponding attribute of the reference person is in this example exactly the same attitude: whether he wanted to be remembered as brilliant student, star athlete, or most popular. The substantive question, then, is this: What effect does a boy who wants to be seen as a brilliant student have in shaping the aspirations of a boy who holds him as a point of reference? (and parallel questions for the boy who aspires to be star athlete, or most popular).

This is nearly a straightforward problem of panel analysis, looking at the mutual effects of two variables by means of data at two points in time. But it differs in one important way, a way which makes for great difficulty in usual punched-card analysis—or even for hand analysis, unless one has had infinite patience. The information required comes not just from a given questionnaire, nor even from the two questionnaires at the two points in spring and fall; it must come also from the questionnaire of the person named. With a computer this variation is a relatively simple one because the computer makes it easy, for the first time, to take into account structures of relationships between people in quantitative analysis. This problem of data analysis leads across a hazy boundary into the area of synthesis, of system simulation, as the next example will indicate.

Example—In What Direction Do Popular Heroes Pull the System? Now suppose we take a slightly different tack toward the problem discussed above. Rather than looking at the simple pairwise relation between the reference person and the person looking up to him, we look at the system as a whole—we ask in what direction it is *moving.* That is, if we consider the reference persons as effecting pulls upon those who look toward them, then the social system as a whole is being pulled in one direction or another. In other words, we are looking at the system as a whole, not just at two persons at a time. Boy c, who is a reference point for a, is himself looking toward h as a point of reference, and h may in turn be looking toward still another boy, n. Instead of a simple pair relation, there is a whole chain, or a set of chains, and instead of examining the "reference point behavior" of individuals, we are examining which way the system is moving.

How is all this accomplished? Though its aim is quite different from the data-analysis problem, it involves only slight modifications of the computer program. We start again with the first individual, find his reference person, and then compare their attitudes—taking as given the actual data at time 1. But now, if the reference person wants to be, say, a star athlete, and the referring person a brilliant student, the referring person's attitude may change or he may drop the reference person. This change is recorded, and the program moves on to the next person. At the end of all persons, the proportions of various changes are calculated. As in the previous example, the effect of the reference person upon the referring one can then be found.

Up to this point, the program has analyzed the effect of this relationship, using data at two time periods. But the program does not stop there. Using the proportions of change as probabilities, it calculates the new hypothetical distribution of attitudes, then replaces the old ones with the new, and starts out again in a new cycle. This new cycle treats the hypothetical attitudes as data, and calculates changes in them, giving rise to a second "new distribution" of attitudes. It then replaces the old attitudes with the new ones, and again cycles through a new time period. The cycles can be continued for as long a simulated time as desired—in this case, until the boy graduates from high school. The over-all program is described in Table 1.

It is important to note one point in this "simulation": Where does the program get the probabilities of change mentioned above? The

Table 1

Outline of Program for Synthesizing the Pull of Reference Person's Attitudes on Person Who Looks to Him.

1. Start with individual *a,* as referring person.
2. Extract digit 9 from referring person's cell in bank *B.*
3. In storage bank C_1, extract identification number of person he wants to be like.
4. Extract digit 9 of this person.
5. Compare the two attitudes, and depending on whether same or different, change either choice or attitude of referring person, with given probabilities.
6. Store this new attitude as digit 8 of referring person, and if choice is changed, wipe out identification number of reference person in referring person's storage in C_1.
7. Go on to individual *b,* and recycle to steps 2 through 6.
8. When finished with all persons, calculate the "new distribution" of attitudes in digit 8.
9. Shift digit 8 to digit 9, and repeat the whole process, steps 1 through 8.
10. Carry each grade through a number of cycles (steps 1 through 9) corresponding to the number of years it has left in school. At each cycle, calculate the "new distribution" of attitudes.

answer is clear in this case: they derive directly from the data analysis of the reference group phenomena. In other words, the data analysis gives us the "weights," or the probabilities, which serve as parameters in the system simulation.

Often, of course, one would not have the second wave, so that these probabilities of change could not be calculated. In such a case, the tactic is to apply *various* hypothetical parameters, and see how the system behaves under the influence of each. When one is comparing several systems (as in this research, I have been comparing different high schools), the parameters may not matter so much—the relative directions in which the different systems move may be roughly the same regardless of the probabilities—one high school moving in an athletic direction, another moving in a scholastic direction.

This example has led into areas which I find particularly exciting. The reason for my excitement is nothing more nor less than this: it opens up possibilities of gathering data on a social system, at one time or preferably two. First we can carry out a data analysis, and then using the *results* of the analysis we can show how the system may be expected to function over a period of time—simulating the processes which operate in a social system so as to see the long-term or indirect changes that might be expected to occur. Is this analysis or synthesis? It is some of both, I would say, and social theory too. As such, it represents what seems to me to be a radically new departure in social research. For the social theory is programed directly into the machine—as the process which makes the simulated system behave as it does.

I want now to turn even further in the direction of simulation and away from data analysis. This final example is one which is pure simulation and as such is designed to answer problems somewhat different from those examined above.

Example—Stability and Instability in Three-Person Groups. Several observers have noted in the literature that a three-person group often seems to be unstable, degenerating into a dyad and an isolate. Let us assume for the present that this is an established fact; that such instability does occur, as the evidence suggests. The question then is, what causes it? It is at this point that the possibility of system simulation comes in. For one can ask this question: If I assume that some process is operating in the group, will this process account for the instability? To answer the question, one can then program the process into the computer, set up a hypothetical situation with an initially balanced three-person group, and then watch what happens over time.

It is important to recognize what is done in such a case. The researcher is not postulating that a group *does* in fact behave this way. He is merely asking whether a particular process can account for the observed regularity.

The specific approach which has been taken is that of Homans, Merton, and many others who have stated the following generalization about people in association: interaction between persons tends to create positive sentiments; these sentiments in turn generate further interaction over and above that initially imposed by external conditions.

If such a process operated among two persons, and each had no other demands on his time, it would lead to ever-increasing interaction until they became inseparable. But life is not like that. In particular, among three persons, A's tendency to interact with B is constrained by his desires to interact with C, and B's and C's desires to interact with one another. As a consequence something must give. The problem raised here is: What will give? If these processes or reinforced interaction operate for all three pairs, will there tend to develop a strong relation between two members and a weak one between each of them and the other? *If this process is operative, and the group starts out completely balanced, will it remain balanced, or will the processes pull it off toward one pair?*

Again it is important to make the problem clear. There is no attempt here to simulate realistically the behavior of a three-person group. The attempt is far more modest. It is to simulate the behavior of three hypothetical persons who act only on one premise. They tend to like more those persons they interact with, and they tend to interact more with persons they like. Collapsing these two relations, they tend to interact more with a person as a result of past interaction. The question, then, is whether such a process can result, over time, in the degeneration of a three-person group into a pair and an isolate.

The general way this is programed on a computer is shown in Figure 1. Each interaction adds to positive or negative sentiments; and these sentiments in turn dictate the chances of interaction between A and B, A and C, and B and C at each unit of time.

The result is not so simple as one might expect. If the system starts out with some past experience so that persons have developed some feelings toward one another, it tends to remain balanced. Although small fluctuations occur, they dampen out before becoming large, so that the system stays nearly balanced.

At the other extreme, there is a situation where sharp imbalance does occur. If the reinforcement for each interaction is quite strong and there is little past experience, then imbalance does occur; a dyad and an isolate frequently result. But there is another kind of imbalance, which is just as frequent: one in which A interacts greatly with B and C, but they interact little with one another.

The result, however, is incidental to the point of the example. The point is this: that "pure" simulation of processes in a social system

Figure 1 Flow chart for stochastic interaction within a triad, depending on rewards and punishments from past interactions.

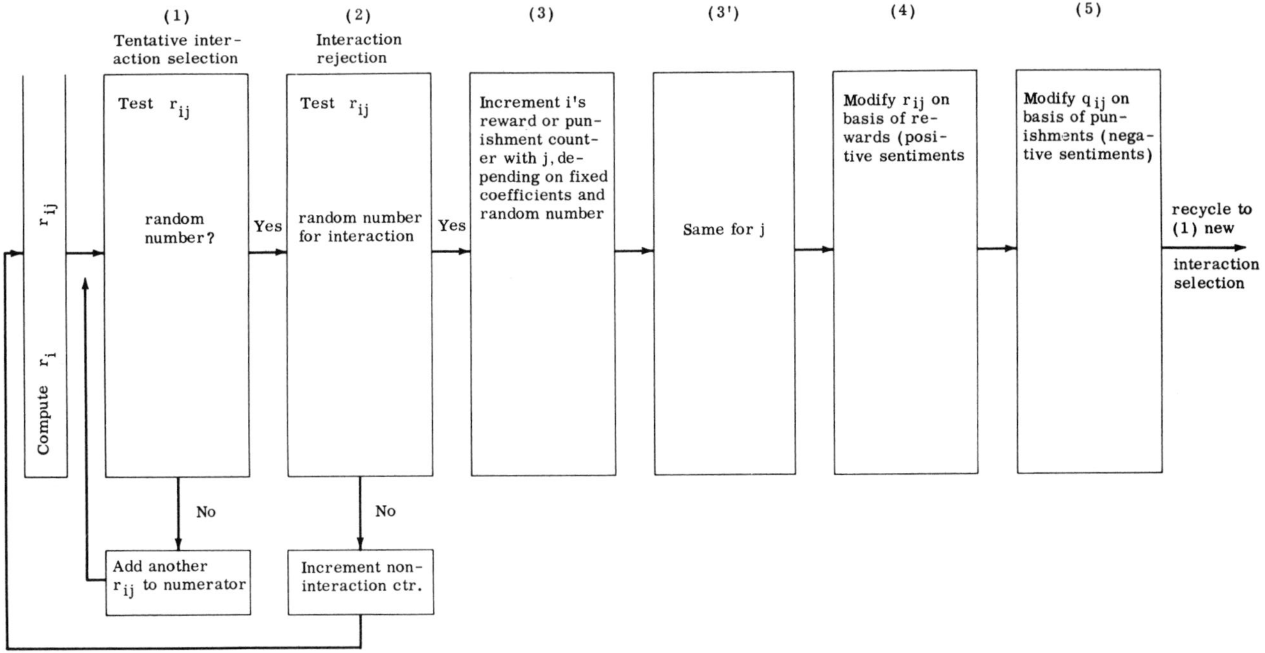

can be valuable for the sociologist. Perhaps simulation is the wrong word, for it suggests that the attempt is to mirror in detail the actual functioning of a social system. Instead, it is very different. The aim is to program into the computer certain theoretical processes, and then to see what kind of a behavior system they generate. The aim is to put together certain processes at the individual and interpersonal level and then to see what consequences they have at the level of the larger system.

6. the simulmatics project

ITHIEL DE SOLA POOL
ROBERT ABELSON

This is the first report on a program of research conducted for the Democratic Party during the 1960 campaign. The research used a new technique for processing poll data and included computer simulation of likely voter behavior. The immediate goal of the project was to estimate rapidly, during the campaign, the probable impact upon the public, and upon small strategically important groups within the public, of different issues which might arise or which might be used by the candidates.

THE DATA

This study is a "secondary analysis" of old poll results. Students of public opinion are becoming aware that the growing backlog of earlier polls provides a powerful tool to aid in the interpretation of new poll results. Polling has now been routine for three decades, but poll archives are just beginning to be assembled. The main one is the Roper Public Opinion Research Center in Williamstown, the existence of which made feasible the project here described.[1]

The first step in the project was to identify in that archive all polls anticipating the elections of 1952, 1954, 1956, and 1958. (Pre-elec-

[1] We wish to express our gratitude to that Center, as well as to the MIT Computation Center, and to the men who originally assembled the data, especially George Gallup and Elmo Roper.

Reprinted in part from Ithiel de Sola Pool and Robert Abelson, "The Simulmatics Project," *The Public Opinion Quarterly*, XXV (1961), 167-183, with the permission of the authors and the Princeton University Press.

This study was carried out by the Simulmatics Corporation.

tion polls on the 1960 contest were added later when they became available.) We selected those polls which contained standard identification data on region, city size, sex, race, socio-economic status, party, and religion, the last being the item most often missing. Further, we restricted our attention to those polls which asked about vote intention and also about a substantial number of pre-selected issues such as civil rights, foreign affairs, and social legislation. From 1952 to 1958 we found fifty usable surveys covering 85,000 respondents. Sixteen polls anticipating the 1960 elections were added to this number. The sixty-six surveys represented a total of well over 100,-000 interviews.

PROCESSING THE DATA

To handle such massive data required substantial innovations in analytic procedures. In essence, the data were reduced to a 480-by-52 matrix. The number 480 represented voter types, each voter type being defined by socio-economic characteristics. A single voter type might be "Eastern, metropolitan, lower-income, white, Catholic, female Democrats." Another might be, "Border state, rural, upper-income, white, Protestant, male Independents." Certain types with small numbers of respondents were reconsolidated, yielding the total of 480 types actually used.

The number 52 represented what we called in our private jargon "issue clusters." Most of these were political issues, such as foreign aid, attitudes toward the United Nations, and McCarthyism. Other so-called "issue clusters" included such familiar indicators of public opinion as "Which party is better for people like you?" vote intention, and nonvoting. In sum, the issue clusters were political characteristics on which the voter type would have a distribution.

One can picture the 480-by-52 matrix as containing four numbers in each cell. The first number stated the total number of persons of that voter type asked about that particular item of information. The other three numbers trichotomized those respondents into the percentages pro, anti, and undecided or confused on the issue.

We assembled such a matrix for each biennial election separately and also a consolidated matrix for all elections together. Thus, it was possible by comparison of the separate matrices to examine trends.

* * *

PURPOSES OF THE METHOD

The reader may wonder what purposes were served by reorganizing the data into the standard format just described. That handling of the data lent itself to three main uses: (1) A "data bank" was available from which one might draw the answer to any one of a vast number of questions at a moment's notice. (2) The consolidation of separate surveys made available adequate data on small, yet politically significant, subsegments in the population. For example, we wrote a report on Northern Negro voters based upon 4,050 interviews, including 418 with middle-class Negroes. The typical national sample survey contains no more than 100 interviews with Northern Negroes, a number clearly inadequate for refined analysis. (3) The data format and its transfer to high-speed tape facilitated its use in computer simulation of the effects of hypothetical campaign strategies.

* * *

SIMULATIONS

We describe, first, how we simulated state-by-state results and, second, how we simulated the impact of the religious issue.

One of the benefits gained from the large number of interviews we used was the possibility of approximating state-by-state results. A national sample survey—even a relatively large one—has too few cases from most states to permit any significant analysis of state politics. The same would have been true, however, even for our voluminous data if we had attempted to do a state-by-state analysis in a simple way. We had an average of about 2,000 interviews per state, but that is a misleading figure. In a small state there might have been no more than 300 or 400 interviews, and on a particular issue cluster that had occurred, for example, in only one-tenth of the surveys, there would be too few cases for effective analysis. We therefore developed a system for creating synthetic, or simulated, states.

By an elaborate analysis of census, poll, and voting data—made more difficult because 1960 census results were not yet available—we developed a set of estimates on the number of persons of each voter type in each state. (Note that since *region* was one of the defining characteristics for the 480 voter types, there were at most only 108 voter types in any given state.) It was assumed that a voter of a given voter type would be identical regardless of the state from which he came. A simulated state therefore consisted of a weighted average of the behaviors of the voter types in that state, the weighting being proportional to the numbers of such persons in that state. For example, we thus assumed that the difference between Maine and New York is not truly a difference between New Yorkers and inhabitants of Maine as such, but a difference in the proportions of different voter types which make up each state. We assumed that an "upper-income Protestant Republican rural white male" was the same in either state, and that a "small-city Catholic Democratic lower-income female" was also the same in either. This assumption enabled us to use all cases of a voter type from a particular region in arriving at a conclusion for a state.

We do not assert that the assumptions on which this simulation is based are true. On the contrary, we can be sure that they are partly false. The interesting question intellectually is how good were the results obtained with these partially true assumptions. The test is, of course, how far state-by-state predictions made on these assumptions turn out to correspond to reality. To the extent that they do, they suggest that the essential differences between states in a region are in distributions of types rather than in geographic differences, even within a voter type.[2]

Upon this simulation of states was built a second and more interesting simulation, one which attempted to assess the impact of the religious issue. Since the one simulation rests upon the other, the effectiveness of the state simulation is simultaneously tested by examination of the religious simulation. The latter, the main simulation actually carried out during the campaign, represented a hypothetical campaign in which the only issues were party and Catholicism. Our report of this simulation was limited to the North because of the peculiar role of party in the South. The outcome was a ranking of thirty-two states ranging from the one in which we estimated Kennedy would do best to the one in which we estimated he would do worst. The ranking was:

---

[2] The states where the simulation was most notably off included Arizona, Nevada, New Mexico, Idaho, and Colorado, states mostly of small population, and states which, in the absence of a "Mountain Region" in our classification, we attempted to treat as Western or Midwestern. Clearly, the assumption of regional uniformity was misleading as applied to them.

1. Rhode Island	17. Pennsylvania
2. Massachusetts	18. Nevada
3. New Mexico	19. Washington
4. Connecticut	20. New Hampshire
5. New York	21. Wyoming
6. Illinois	22. Oregon
7. New Jersey	23. North Dakota
8. California	24. Nebraska
9. Arizona	25. Indiana
10. Michigan	26. South Dakota
11. Wisconsin	27. Vermont
12. Colorado	28. Iowa
13. Ohio	29. Kansas
14. Montana	30. Utah
15. Minnesota	31. Idaho
16. Missouri	32. Maine

The product-moment correlation over states between the Kennedy index on the simulation (not strictly speaking a per cent) and the actual Kennedy vote in the election was .82. It should be emphasized that this satisfying result was based upon political data not a single item of which was later than October 1958. Surveys on the 1960 election were not available soon enough to be incorporated into this analysis.

The basic method in this simulation was a fairly straightforward application of the cross-pressure findings of earlier election studies.[3] These findings enabled us to improve our estimate of how a particular voter will behave if we know the cross-pressures he is under. With such knowledge, an analyst should feel more comfortable making guesses about how voters under particular kinds of cross-pressure will shift in an election than he would about making an over-all intuitive guess at the outcome. The method of this simulation was to make a series of such detailed estimates and then let the computer put them together to give an over-all outcome.

To make these detailed estimates we classified our set of 480 voter types into 9 possible cross-pressure subsets arising from a 3-by-3 breakdown on religion and party: Protestants, Catholics and others; Republicans, Democrats and Independents. For each of the nine resulting situations we made a prediction. For example, take the Protestant Republicans. They were not under cross-pressure. Since

---

[3] Bernard R. Berelson, Paul F. Lazarsfeld, William N. McPhee, *Voting: A Study of Opinion Formation in a Presidential Campaign* (Chicago: University of Chicago Press, 1954).

our data had revealed no substantial dislike of Nixon as an individual among such voters, we saw no reason why their vote in 1960 should differ substantially from their vote in 1956, even though Eisenhower was not running. Thus for them we wrote two equations:

$$V_k = P_{56} \ (1 - P_{35})$$
$$V_n = Q_{56} \ (1 - P_{35})$$

meaning that the predicted Kennedy percentage (V_k) in any voter type of this Protestant-Republican sort would be the percentage of persons in that voter type who had indicated a preference for Stevenson in the 1956 polls (P_{56}), reduced by the nonvoting record of that voter type ($1 - P_{35}$).[4] The equation for the expected Nixon percentage (V_n) was the same except that it used the 1956 Eisenhower supporters (Q_{56}).

The above was the simplest set of equations used. Let us now turn to a more complicated set, that for a group under cross-pressure—Protestant Democrats. First, we decided that, barring the religious issue, 1958 vote intentions would be a better index of the Protestant Democrats' 1960 vote than would their 1956 vote intentions. Too many of them were Eisenhower defectors in 1956 for us to believe that 1956 was a good indicator of normal behavior. On the other hand, 1958 polls would overestimate their Democratic vote, since many of them would defect again against a Catholic. However, it would not suffice merely to subtract the percentage who gave anti-Catholic replies on poll questions, for perhaps those very Democrats who were anti-Catholic were the ones who in practice voted Republican anyway. In short, the question was: Were the bigot defectors right wingers whose vote the Democrats would lose even without a Catholic candidate? Our system could not give us that information for each respondent incorporated into our data. While one respondent in a voter type might have been polled in a survey in 1958 about his vote intentions, another man of the same voter type, on a different survey, might have been polled on whether he would vote for a Catholic for President. To estimate the correlation between these two variables we had to find one or more surveys on which both questions appeared. We then ran anti-Catholicism by 1958 vote for each of the

---

[4] Since we trichotomized results, $P_{56} + Q_{56}$ do not add up to 100 per cent. The reader may wonder why a turnout correction is added: are not the residuals the nonvoters? The answer is that a turnout correction is needed because many more persons express a candidate preference on a poll than actually turn out to vote.

more numerous Protestant Democrat voter types. We found that among them the ratio ad/bc in the following fourfold table averaged about .6. With that information we could estimate how many of the anti-Catholics were hopeless cases anyhow (i.e., had gone Republican even in 1958) and how many would be net losses only in a campaign dominated by the religious issue.

1958 Vote Intentions	Anti-Catholic	Not Anti-Catholic
Democratic	a	b
Republican	c	d

It should be added here that we decided to take poll replies on the religious issue at face value. We were not so naïve as to believe that this was realistic, but since we were not trying to predict absolute percentages, but only relative ones, all that mattered was that the true extent of anti-Catholicism, voter type by voter type, should be linearly related to the percentage overtly expressed. Even this could only be assumed as a promising guess.

Finally, in predicting the vote of the Protestant Democrat voter types, we took account of the established finding that voters under cross-pressure stay home on election day more often than voters whose pressures are consistent. Therefore, for our 1960 estimate we doubled the historically established nonvoting index for these types.

Thus we arrived at equations applied to each Protestant Democratic voter type:

$$V_k = (P_{58} - a) \ (1 - 2P_{35})$$
$$V_n = (Q_{58} + a) \ (1 - 2P_{35})$$

The estimate of anti-Catholic 1958 Democratic voters (i.e., persons in cell a in the fourfold table above) was arrived at by the computer, given that

$$a + b = P_{58} \qquad a + c = P_{14} \ (P_{58} + Q_{58})$$

$$P_{14} = \text{per cent anti-Catholic} \qquad \text{and} \ \frac{ad}{bc} = .6$$

Space precludes a similar examination of each of the other of the nine conditions. Suffice it to say that one other set of serious guesses had to be made, namely what proportion of those Democratic Catholics who had voted Republican in 1958 would switch back to their party to vote for Kennedy and what proportion of Republican Catholics who had voted Republican in 1958 would also switch to Ken-nedy. After an examination of the trial-heat data from polls which asked about Kennedy vs. Nixon, we decided to use one-third as the proportion in each case, and to use that figure also as an estimate of the proportion of Catholic independents who would be won back by the religious issue.

The simulation required that the computer make 480 separate calculations, each one using the appropriate set of equations from above. During each of the 480 calculations, the computer put into the equations values for turnout record, 1958 vote intention, 1956 vote intention, and anti-Catholicism, derived from the data which had been assembled about that particular voter type. This gave a 1960 vote estimate for each voter type for the particular hypothetical cam-paign being investigated. Weighted averages of these gave the state-by-state estimates.

These estimates, as we have already noted, turned out to be close to the actual November outcome. They were not intended to be predictions. Or, rather, they were *contingent* predictions only. They were predictions of what would happen *if* the religious issue domi-nated the campaign. We did not predict that this would happen. We were describing one out of a set of possible types of campaign situ-ation. But by August, when we took our national survey, comparison of our simulation and the survey results showed that this situation was actually beginning to occur. And the closeness of our contingent prediction to the final November result suggests that, indeed, the religious issue was of prime importance.

How close was the religious-issue simulation to the actual outcome compared to alternative bases of prediction? A full exploration of this remains to be made. We must, for example, further vary the param-eters used in the simulation to determine which ones affect the results most critically and which values of those give the best pre-diction. For the present we look only at the one set of values and equations on which we relied during the campaign and which has already been described. (A few variations were tried and dismissed during the campaign, but none that made much difference.) How did this one simulation compare with other predictive data?

An obvious comparison is with the Kennedy-Nixon trial heats on polls taken at the same time as the latest polls used in the simulation. The correlation between the state-by-state result of these polls and the actual outcome is but .53 as compared to .82 for the simulation.

The simulation, in short, portrayed trends which actually took place between the time the data were collected and election day. The uncorrected polls two years before the election explained but one-fourth of the variance in the real results, while intelligent use of them taking into account the cross-pressure theory of voting behavior allowed us to explain nearly two-thirds of the variance.

A more stringent comparison would be with Kennedy-Nixon trial heats run in August 1960, when the simulation was run on the computer. Such a comparison would answer the question of whether the Democratic Party would have gotten as good information at that date by the conventional means of up-to-the-minute field interviewing as it got by reanalysis of old data. Very likely it could have, if it had chosen to invest in a large enough national sample survey to give it state-by-state results, for as far as we can now tell the Catholic issue exerted most of its impact by shortly after the conventions. However, until poll data for that period becomes available we can only speculate. We wish to emphasize, however, that at some point in the history of the campaign, poll data certainly came into close correlation with the November election results and thus with our simulation. The date the raw poll results became as or more predictive than the simulation would be the point in the campaign at which mechanisms of voter behavior anticipated in the simulation became reality.

Besides simulation and polls, what other indices might have forecast long in advance the state-by-state order of voting in 1960? Results of previous elections would be one such index. Perhaps the rank order of the states in a previous election is a good forecast of rank order in future ones, even if the electoral outcome changes. (The whole country could move one way or the other, leaving the order of the states much the same.) But, if one is to use this device, which election should one use? The year 1956 was a presidential election year, as was 1960, but in 1956 the Eisenhower phenomenon was operating. 1958, although more recent and less affected by Eisenhower's idiosyncratic appeal, was a Congressional election year. In our simulation, too, we faced this problem. We resolved it for some voter types one way, for some another. But what happens if one relies on a single simple over-all assumption of continuity between elections? The result is not very good, though slightly better using 1956 than 1958. The product-moment correlation of Northern results between 1956 and 1960 was .39, between 1958 and 1960, .37. The multiple correlation using both earlier years was .44 with the 1960 election. So far our simulation clearly was superior as a forecast.

Perhaps one might have made a good prediction of the impact of the religious issue by a simple slide-rule method of calculation instead of by an elaborate computer procedure. One could correct the 1956 or 1958 vote by some crude percentage of the Catholic population of each state. That would have worked and worked well if, by some act of intuitive insight, one could have hit on the right percentage correction. One would have had to decide first of all to use 1956, not 1958, as the base, for no simple correction of the 1958 results gives a good correlation with the actual outcome. If one had that correct flash of intuition, one could have surpassed our complex simulation with a correction of exactly 34 per cent of the Catholic percentage of the population added to the Democratic vote. The correlation with the actual outcome achieved by this process is .83. The simulation was better, however, than any correction except 34 per cent. It is better than 33 or 35 per cent. At corrections of 32 and 40 per cent the coefficients of correlation for the simple correction procedure drop below .80.

There was, in other words, a "lucky guess" way of estimating the effect of the religious issue in the campaign which would have given an excellent prediction. But even if we had tried to make such an over-all estimate and had somehow arrived at the right "lucky guess," we could not have defended it against skeptics. What the simulation did was to allow competent political analysts, operating without inspired guesses, to make sober, scientifically explicable estimates that they were willing to commit to paper before the facts. As the accompanying table shows, the simulation gave results about as good as the very best which *hindsight* now tells us could have been reached by simpler methods if infused by the right lucky guesses.

CORRELATIONS WITH ACTUAL ELECTION RESULTS

Trial heats contemporaneous with simulation data	.53
Continuity with 1956	.39
Continuity with 1958	.37
Continuity with 1956 and 1958	.44
1956 results with optimum, or "lucky guess," correction for Catholic vote	.83
Simulation as done during campaign	.82

The essence of the simulation was to treat each voter type separately. Under what conditions should one expect that procedure to obtain a better result than an optimal across-the-board correction applied to the total? Clearly, if the process at work in each voter type was uniform it would make no difference whether we applied correction factors voter type by voter type or to the total. One could add 34 per cent of each Catholic voter type to the Democratic vote for that type or add 34 per cent of total Catholics to the total Democratic vote and come out with the same result. Where there are complex interactions of several variables on a voter type, however, then calculations done the two ways are no longer equal. If, for example, turnout varies between voter types and party voting also varies, then an equation applied to each voter type could not equally well be applied to total voters.

It is clear that we did not use the most predictive values for all parameters in our simulation. Determining what these were with the aid of hindsight is part of our present research program. But before election day we had no way of knowing what they were. (The one-third of 1958 Catholics casting Republican votes likely to go Democratic in 1960 according to our equations should not be confused with the 34 per cent of all 1956 Catholic voters, which turned out to be a good across-the-board correction.) The fact that our result came out on a par with the optimum simple correction which hindsight has enabled us to make is a crude measure of the gain from working voter type by voter type, with account taken of interactions within each type, that is, the gain from the computer operations.

The test of any new method of research is successful use. The outcome of the present study gives reason to hope that computer simulation may indeed open up the possibility of using survey data in ways far more complex than has been customary in the past. The political "pros" who commissioned this abstruse study were daring men to gamble on the use of a new and untried technique in the heat of a campaign. The researchers who undertook this job faced a rigorous test, for they undertook to do both basic and applied research at once. The study relied upon social science theories and data to represent the complexity of actual human behavior to a degree that would permit the explicit presentation of the consequences of policy alternatives.

This kind of research could not have been conducted ten years ago. Three new elements have entered the picture to make it possible: first, a body of sociological and psychological theories about voting and other decisions; second, a vast mine of empirical survey data now for the first time available in an archive; third, the existence of high-speed computers with large memories. The social science theories allow us to specify with some confidence what processes will come to work in a decision situation. The backlog of survey data permits us to estimate the parameters of these processes with fair precision and great detail for each small element of our national population. The computer makes possible the handling of this mine of data. More important still, it makes possible the precise carrying out of long and complex chains of reasoning about the interactions among the different processes. In summary, we believe that conditions now exist for use of survey data in research far more ambitious than social scientists are used to. If it is possible to reproduce, through computer simulation, much of the complexity of a whole society going through processes of change, and to do so rapidly, then the opportunities to put social science to work are vastly increased. It is our belief that this is now possible which was put to a test by the campaign research reported here.

7. a use of simulation
in the study of inter-nation relations

HAROLD GUETZKOW
Northwestern University

Events, as recorded in all their variety in historical and contemporary documents, are the usual basis for the development of theory about relations among nations. These international events our theory must explain, and these events we eventually hope to predict. Such theory building—consisting of the development of adequate concepts and the relations of these concepts to each other in propositions—must encompass the welter of facts from life situations. Our theories of international relations—be they implicit or explicit—are the stuff from which we compose our policies, and write our newspapers and textbooks. This essay describes an initial effort to utilize simulation techniques as complementary means both for the development of theory and for instructional purposes.[1]

[1] Early plans for the simulation were thought through during my stay at the Center for Advanced Study in the Behavioral Sciences. The three exploratory runs reported in this paper were supported in 1957-58 by funds from the Carnegie Corporation of New York. My colleagues and students at Northwestern made many suggestions during the seminars devoted to the formulation of these runs. Professors Richard C. Snyder, George I. Blanksten, and R. Barry Farrell personally participated in the early trial run. Mr. Denis A. Sullivan shared some of the preliminary results from his inventory of propositions in international relations, which further helped guide my selection of key variables. But above all, full credit must go to Mr. Robert C. Noel for developing the mechanics of the simulation in a most creative way, never allowing theoretical objectives to be swamped by practical necessities.

Reprinted in part from Harold Guetzkow, "A Use of Simulation in the Study of Inter-Nation Relations," *Behavioral Science*, 4 (1959), 183-191, with the permission of the Mental Health Research Institute, The University of Michigan.

Simulation is an operating representation of central features of reality. Simulations may take the form of war games, of pilot chemical plants, of ship-and-harbor scale models, of computer-inventory systems. There are a multitude of such representations (Malcolm, 1958). Will a social simulation of inter-nation relations prove to be of value as a heuristic device for theory development in international relations research? May inter-nation simulation be arranged to allow live participants to play component units for training purposes? Three exploratory runs of an inter-nation simulation in the laboratory of the Program of Graduate Training and Research in International Relations at Northwestern University in 1957-58 suggest that simulation technique may be useful for purposes of both research and training.

BACKGROUND FOR SIMULATION

The efforts in simulation at Northwestern were stimulated by two streams of intellectual endeavor, one represented in the war game and the other deriving from the social psychological group experiment. . . .

The immediate impetus for explorations in simulation came from the author's work in the social psychology of groups. Since the 1930's, experimental psychologists and sociologists have developed face-to-face groups in laboratories to test theories of group interaction (Cartwright and Zander, 1953; Hare, Borgatta and Bales, 1955). This work with contrived face-to-face groups has been elaborated in the laboratory study of organizations with component parts at both the Graduate School of Industrial Administration at Carnegie Institute of Technology (Guetzkow and Bowes, 1957) and at the Case Institute of Technology. An inter-nation simulation may be thought of as another step in the construction of social systems, the contriving of an inter-organizational system.

But the deeper source for this work is found in the developments in decision-making, as exemplified in the work of Simon and Snyder. Simon and his colleagues developed their interests in decision-making from the perspective of public and, later, private administration (Simon, Smithburg and Thompson, 1950; March and Simon, with Guetzkow, 1958). Snyder and his colleagues developed their ideas from the perspective of decision-making in foreign politics (Snyder, Bruck and Sapin, 1954; Snyder, 1958).

DESCRIPTION OF THE INTER-NATION SIMULATION

Contrived face-to-face groups, even when they are created in the experimenter's laboratory, are more replications of reality than they are simulations. The component units—that is, the persons participating in the experiment—necessarily respond to their social environment as human beings even though the environment may be artificially simplified. In the war game, however, there is more role-playing, in which the actors need to imagine many features of the military situation and respond to each other's moves in terms of these self-imposed role conceptions. Usually there is time compression, so that, for example, a month's warfare may be enacted within a day. The mechanical and civil engineer often builds his simulation by reducing his phenomena in scale. The operations research analyst represents the flow of traffic in symbolic form, so that he may use digits in a computer as simulation of a distribution of vehicles. In making such an analogue, there often is simplification, as when traffic is allowed only to turn left or right, even though vehicles in reality can make U-turns. All these devices have been used in developing the inter-nation simulation. We have attempted to represent social units— nations, in this case—in their inter-relations with each other. We have simplified and reduced the number of variables involved. We have used both analogies and replication in contriving the parts. *Our simulation is an operating representation in reduced and/or simplified form of relations among social units by means of symbolic and/or replicate component parts.*

When one builds literary and mathematical models, one makes choices as to which features of a system are to be represented (Guetzkow, 1958a). When building social simulations, such choices also must be made. One is forced to specify units and interrelations which often may be left abstract and general in verbal models. The concreteness to be embodied in this description of the inter-nation simulation must not be taken seriously. As the work proceeds, revisions necessarily will make the representation more satisfactory. Eventually, variations will be introduced in order to check effects of different forms of the simulation. The choice of variables and the representation of their interlocking is highly tentative.

five nations and their two decision-makers

In the three initial, exploratory runs described in this paper, five "nations" were operated simultaneously. During the first run, the nations were manned by one, or two, or three decision-makers. Those three units operated by one participant tended to be outward oriented, with less attention given to internal considerations. The nation which was operated by three decision-makers became quite bogged down in its internal processes, so that it had little time left for inter-state interactions. The unit manned by two decision-makers seemed balanced in its orientations. In the second and third runs, each nation was manned by two participants, senior and graduate students concentrating in political science.

In each unit, then, an "internal decision-maker" (IDM) made the nation's final decisions with regard to overall policies of the nation as they related to both external and internal considerations. Another participant served as "external decision-maker" (EDM), conducting the relations of his unit with other nations. The EDM reported to the IDM and might have been replaced by the latter. Yet, some IDMs used their EDMs as collaborators in their decisions. The two positions attempt to represent decision-making as it encompasses the nation as a whole, especially as the government relates to its resources and society, and as the nation relates to an external environment, consisting of other nations.

office holding

Considerable effort was made to embed the external decisions in the internal environment. The decision-makers were under pressure to maintain themselves in office. Office holding depended upon the extent to which the expectations of the nation's validators (e.g., citizens, elites, juntas, and other forces which maintain decision-makers in office) were met. The probability of being maintained in office depended upon calculations made by the researchers as to how well both external and internal goals were being achieved by the nation in question. At the end of three periods of decision-making, the retention or loss of office was ascertained in each nation on the basis of random determinations (with the probability set as the average of the probabilities obtained for each period). By averaging probabilities, the decision-makers were able to take long-range points of view in making decisions which might decrease their momentary chances for office holding. Such a situation typically occurs in electoral processes in which there is delayed response to official actions. When the probability of office holding, however, decreased to specified critical levels, an immediate determination was calculated, even though the routine determination was still some periods off. Such consequences simulated revolutions and coup d'états.

nation-goals

In the experiment each nation attempted to accomplish its goals, which then served as a basis for its decisions. In two of the runs, the goals were formulated by the decision-makers themselves; in the third simulation, goals were assigned to the IDMs by the researchers. Goals included objectives such as security, domination, cooperation, and internal growth.

resource decisions

Each nation periodically received basic resources which it could allocate to its internal functioning or utilize in external affairs, either as aid or as strategic strength. Its internal use of these resources could be distributed to its validators for immediate gratification or for building up basic resources during the coming periods. These decisions were recorded on a decision-form by the IDMs, so that they might serve as one of the bases for computation of the probability of office holding.

interaction among nations

Once each nation had its preliminary goals and had learned how to make its decisions with regard to its resources, the simulation was put into operation. Besides bi-lateral interaction, the EDMs arranged for conferences of some or all of the nations, with and without their IDMs. The EDMs made treaties, giving aid with or without restrictions. The strategic strength of the nation was used for various purposes, including intimidation of other nations. It was possible for one nation to declare war upon another, alone or within alliances. Some nations endeavored to build permanent forms of international cooperation. As the interaction developed, the nations were allowed to reformulate their goals.

In the first exploratory run, there were direct communications among the EDMs in bilateral contacts and at conferences. However, to insure perspective on the total scene by the decision-makers, it was useful to create a communication system beyond the one established by the EDMs. During the second and third runs, an external communications system was devised by the researchers in which events were reported to all nations, so that there was more understanding by the decision-makers of what was happening within the interaction system. In this "world newspaper," reports were made by the researchers on the office losses as they occurred, how aid was extended, how treaties and alliances were developed. In addition, the EDMs were permitted to publish communiqués and announcements for propaganda purposes.

laboratory mechanics

The group laboratory of Northwestern's Departments of Psychology and Sociology was used for the experiment, as pictured in Figure 1. Although all the participants were physically proximate,

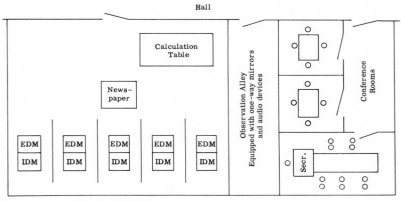

Hall

Participants' Tables
EDM and IDM separated by barrier.
Tables separated by floor screens.

Figure 1　Group laboratory, Northwestern University.

only written communications were permitted, to allow the researchers to obtain a complete record of the transactions. Within a nation, the IDM and EDM passed messages back and forth by sliding them through the barrier separating the two halves of the table at which they were seated. Nonparticipating messengers carried the inter-nation messages from one EDM to another. Carbons of all messages were given to the researcher-reporter, so that reports for the newspaper could be prepared from those not marked "RESTRICTED." The nations were shielded from each other by screens.

The conferences were conducted at round tables, with various methods of recording. In small conferences, the decision-makers simply passed a sheet of paper back and forth, with all reading the last reply before the next response was begun. In larger conferences, a blackboard in view of all was used for the interchanges. A record was made of the messages immediately, so that each EDM might have a copy of the conference transcript.

An hour was allowed for each period of the simulation. Half-way through the period, the IDMs completed the decision-forms, so that the researchers might use them in calculating the probabilities of office holding. The consequences of their decisions were returned to the decision-makers at the beginning of the following period.

In calculating the outcomes, the researchers used a combination of rigid rules and subjective judgments. For example, the strength of states was mechanically determined from their strategic strength allocations, as combined through their alliances. On the other hand, subjective judgments were made by the simulation director as to how well the nation was achieving its evolving goals. These various measures were then combined into a single validator satisfaction measure, in terms of which office holding was determined mathematically.

No attempt is made in this description to give all the details of the simulation in its full concreteness. Only when the design of the simulation settles into more permanent form will it be useful to report with such elaboration. It is hoped that the description above enables the reader to picture the operations. Once we begin using the simulation for particular training or research purposes, it will be necessary, of course, to specify the details. The three runs, each lasting from three to four hours, indicate some hope of simulating inter-nation relations in the laboratory.

SIMULATION AS MODEL BUILDING

It is believed that inter-nation simulation will be of heuristic value in clarifying our theories of international relations. Although it is but one of alternative ways of building models about the operation of social systems, its operating character demands a greater clarity in formulation than is often necessitated in literary and mathematical formulations.

To construct an operable representation, one must specify variables with some precision and then interlock the variables with some exactitude. So that the participants and researchers can operate the model at a scale reduced from that of the original being simulated, a limited number of key variables must be selected. One attempts to represent a whole class of variables, such as the economic, by a more limited set of prototypic ones. To provide feedback from the decisions to the decision-makers, one simply must specify the interlocking which exists among the variables—otherwise there will be no inter-relation.

As in models which present verbal structures isomorphic to the phenomena being studied, one often has characteristics hidden within the interstices of the model. Because we are using human beings as decision-makers, they bring both their personal characteristics into the model and their own implicit theories of the way in which nations should behave. Eventually it will be necessary to appraise these personal styles of decision-making and organizational presuppositions, so that their influence on the evolving inter-nation interaction may be studied. In one of our exploratory runs, the presence of a decision-maker with a particularly strong interest in dominating other nations was as determinate as the presence, in another run, of a decision-maker who wanted to implement morality standards through development of an international organization.

Perhaps the heuristic values of simulation may be increased by underspecifying parts of the model. To date, our strategy has been to build a well structured base for the decisions made within each nation, but to leave the structuring of inter-nation relations ambiguous. Then the interaction generated in the simulation may evolve characteristics of an inter-nation system which are quite independent of the conscious expectations of both the participants and the researchers. It was interesting to note in one run how the demands of the simulated operation forced the development of a clearer division of labor between IDM and EDM than either wanted. Will the development of the inter-nation system force supra-state organization, above and beyond the nations themselves, when we allow the simulation to continue for ten to fifteen hours instead of cutting it short at three or four?

It would be feasible to put the calculation of the decision consequences on computers, as is done in the business game of the American Management Association (Ricciardi and Craft, 1957). Should the translation of the decisions into office holding probabilities be made more complicated, it may be necessary to do this. Oliver Benson has developed an all-computer simulation called "A Simple Diplomatic Game" (1958). Using an IBM 650 Stored Program Computer, Benson is developing a generalized game involving four preparatory sets of input data, "national power," "interest in other states," the propensity of each of nine powers to act, and geographic location. Nine action decisions may then be fed into the machine, which is programed to compute a set of consequences, as well as "counter-actions." Our simulation differs from both the AMA Business Game and Benson's Diplomatic Game in that our development allows the participants to create consequences as they derive from their inter-group interaction, quite free of programs in the computer.

One of the puzzles encountered in using simulation involving human decision-makers is the extent to which the representation shades into the phenomenon itself. In experimental work with small groups, the social psychologist actually produces face-to-face relations. One would expect in such laboratory replication of the phenomena a surer prediction to the world of nature than when one depends upon the formal isomorphism employed in a simulation. Yet, by using human components—by contriving nations as units which actually interact—to what extent has this simulation become an exemplification of the phenomena themselves? But no matter, for when models developed in simulation predict important features of real inter-nation systems, the distinction becomes of little consequence.

Perhaps most exciting is the potential which simulation models hold for exploration of contemporary verbal theories about international relations. It is feasible to simulate such characteristics as variation in size of nation, representing small and great powers in the same interaction system. It is possible to so structure the simulation as to have nations with rapid growth and slow growth in interaction with each other. We have an impressive literature which can provide hypotheses for examination within the inter-nation simulation.

For instance, we might study the proposition by Haas and Whiting that although "the majority of alliances are concluded for purposes of self-preservation, the dynamics of international relations often transform them into pacts of self-extension for at least one of the parties" (1956, p. 162). By examining the messages of the EDMs, we may understand the arguments used in persuading other nations to join alliances. Then, once established, we can check the extent to which the alliance now is used for self-extension. Consider Kennan's hypothesis, that international "conflicts are to be effectively isolated and composed" the more accurate the perception of the given power relationships surrounding the conflict (1954, p. 36). By asking our decision-makers to record their perceptions of power among the units, we can check whether accuracy in such perceptions does lead to more adequate conflict management in the simulation. Because of the costly nature of simulation, it will be wise to explore a number of related hypotheses simultaneously. For example, while one is working Kennan's hypothesis, it would be feasible, by varying the number of nations, to check Kaplan's notion that "mistakes or failure in information can be tolerated more easily if the number of actors is greater" (1957, p. 34).

Gradually tighter bodies of verbal theory are being developed. One might use simulation for exploring these verbal constructions. For example, the theory of political integration created by Van Wagenen and Deutsch and their colleagues at the Center for Research on World Political Institutions might be mirrored in simulation. Would their prediction of a pluralistic security-community among the nations be realized when conditions of mutual responsiveness to each other's needs are simulated? (Deutsch *et al.,* 1957, p. 66). Or explore Guetzkow's hypothesis that "the more adequately the members of a group envision the techniques of inter-group collaboration as means to their ends, the greater the tendency to move toward collaboration." (1957, p. 54). It would seem feasible to explore Kaplan's constructs of state systems, such as the hierarchical system, even though no exemplification of this phase exists at present in nature. Benson has utilized Quincy Wright's "propensity-to-act" notions in his all-computer simulation.

Once we settle upon a particular design for the inter-nation simulation, it will be feasible to represent the assembly of existent nations. First, one would need to characterize each of these nations on the present variables which are incorporated into the simulation. Using these characterizations as initial conditions, the simulation might be operated, generating consequences—that is, predictions of the evolution of the present international system.

It would seem, however, undesirable—in the present stage of underdevelopment of simulation—to attempt to have our participants role-play particular countries, such as Spain and Indonesia. Would not such encouragement toward role-playing tend to secure reactions in terms of the presuppositions each participant has as to the nature of a particular country's reactions in a foreign policy situation? Then, as was done in the RAND exercise, we would be embodying our participant's theories of how nations are supposed to react rather than exploring reactions produced by the interaction itself.

USE OF SIMULATION FOR TRAINING

An inter-nation simulation may prove useful for training purposes in a number of situations (Guetzkow, 1958b). It may be used as exercise material in the training of policy-makers, and it may complement texts and lectures in the teaching of international relations to undergraduate and graduate students.

As the war game has been judged of practical value in providing decision-maker experience to military executives, so the manning of an inter-nation simulation may be helpful in the training of foreign policy makers. The business decision-game, developed by the American Management Association, is found useful for certain levels of management training, especially as it allows specialized executives to gain over-all perspectives.[2] It was just in this respect that the RAND political exercise was thought to have been most fruitful. Goldsen reports, "The game puts a premium on the mobilization and reordering of preexisting knowledge in relation to a special focus, a focus on political action, policy thinking . . . and the analytic assessments of the consequences of alternative courses of action. Seeing new interconnections of earlier insights . . . seems to have been considerably fostered by the game . . ." (1956, p. 36). The inter-nation simulation, used in conjunction with substantive training in foreign policy, could provide quasi-practical experiences in the exercise of policy judgment. By making explicit that which is often implicit, the simulation would encourage the use of more sophisticated decision-making procedures. Because the simulation could be arranged to provide a constant bombardment of decision-events, practice in decision-making under continuous pressure might be obtained from its use by policy officers preparing for heavy interaction situations. Perhaps the internation simulation can be developed as an adjunct to the case materials being used in the career development programs for foreign service officers in our Foreign Service Institute.

references

Alger, C. F., Personal communication.
Benson, O., *A Simple Diplomatic Game* (Norman: University of Oklahoma, August, 1958). 4 pp. mimeo.

---

[2] We are grateful for the many courtesies of Mr. Virgil Kraft in allowing us full access to their simulation without cost.

Cartwright, D. D. and A. Zander, eds., *Group Dynamics: Research and Theory* (Evanston, Ill.: Row, Peterson, 1953).

Deutsch, K. W., S. A. Burrell, R. A. Kann, M. Lee, Jr., M. Lichterman, R. E. Lindgren, F. L. Loewenheim, and R. W. Van Wagenen, *Political Community and the North Atlantic Area: International Organization in the Light of Historical Experience* (Princeton: Princeton University Press, 1957).

Goldsen, J. M., *The Political Exercise, an Assessment of the Fourth Round* (Washington, D. C., The RAND Corporation, D-3640-RC, May 30, 1956), 59 pp., mimeographed document.

Guetzkow, H., "Building Models About Small Groups," in R. Young, ed., *Approaches to the Study of Politics* (Evanston, Ill.: Northwestern University Press, 1958), pp. 265-281. (a)

———, "Isolation and Collaboration: A Partial theory of inter-nation relations," *Conflict Resolution*, 1957, 1, 48-68.

———, "Training for Policy-Making Roles Through Organizational Simulation," *Proceedings, 14th Annual Conference, American Society of Training Directors*, May 1958), pp. 76-79. (b)

———, and Anne E. Bowes, "The Development of Organizations in a Laboratory," *Management Science*, 1957, 3, 380-402.

Haas, E. B., and A. S. Whiting, *Dynamics of International Relations* (New York: McGraw-Hill Book Co., Inc., 1956).

Hare, E. A. P., E. F. Borgatta, and R. F. Bales, eds., *Small Groups: Studies in Social Interaction* (New York: Alfred A. Knopf, Inc., 1955).

Kaplan, M. A., *System and Process in International Politics* (New York: John Wiley & Sons, Inc., 1957).

Kennan, G. F., *Realities of American Foreign Policy* (Princeton: Princeton University Press, 1954).

Malcolm, D. G., ed., *Report of System Simulation Symposium* (New York: American Institute of Industrial Engineers and co-sponsored by the Institute of Management Sciences and Operations Research Society of America, 1958).

March, J. G., and H. A. Simon, with H. Guetzkow, *Organizations* (New York: John Wiley & Sons, Inc., 1958).

Ricciardi, F. M. and C. J. Craft, *Top Management Decision-Simulation: The AMA Approach* (New York: American Management Association, 1957).

Simon, H. A., D. W. Smithburg, and V. A. Thompson, *Public Administration* (New York: Alfred A. Knopf, Inc., 1950).

Snyder, R. C., "A Decision-Making Approach to the Study of Political Phenomena," in Young, ed., *Approaches to the Study of Politics* (Evanston, Ill.: Northwestern University Press, 1958, pp. 3-38).

———, H. W. Bruck, and B. Sapin, *Decision-Making as an Approach to the Study of International Politics* (Foreign Policy Analysis Project, Princeton University, 1954).

8. simulation of economic systems

GUY H. ORCUTT*

INTRODUCTION

Simulation is a general approach to the study and use of models. As such it furnishes an alternative approach to that offered by conventional mathematical techniques. In using conventional mathematical techniques to solve a model the objective is to determine, deductively and with generality, the way in which the model implicitly relates endogenous variables to initial conditions, parameters, and time paths of exogenous variables.[1]

Simulation techniques also are used to solve models, but in any single simulation run the solution obtained is highly specific. Given completely specified initial conditions, parameters, and exogenous variables, a single simulation run yields only a single set of time paths of the endogenous variables. To determine how the behavior of the endogenous variables is more generally dependent on initial conditions, parameters, and exogenous variables may require a very large number of simulation runs; and even then induction from specific results to general solutions will be required.

An individual simulation run may be thought of as an experiment

---

[1] For purposes of this paper variables generated by a model will be regarded as endogenous, while variables treated as given and fed into a model will be regarded as exogenous. No distinction is made in this paper between constants and parameters.

Reprinted in part from Guy Orcutt, "Simulation of Economic Systems," *The American Economic Review,* L (1960), 893-907, with the permission of the author and the American Economic Association.

* The author wishes to express his appreciation to Janet Fisher and John Korbel for assistance in preparation of this article.

performed upon a model. A given experiment involves operating a model after first completely specifying a set of initial conditions appropriate to the model, a set of values of the parameters used in specifying relations contained in the model, and the time paths of those variables used in the model and treated as exogenous. Additional experiments would involve operating the model after respecifying the initial conditions, the parameters, and/or the exogenous variables. The problem of inferring general relationships from specific results obtained in individual experiments performed on a model is the same as that of inferring general relationships from specific experimental results in any of the inductive sciences. The scientist studying natural phenomena has no alternative. The research worker, studying or using a model, could conceivably use a purely deductive approach, but this alternative may not be attractive or it may not prove feasible with known mathematical methods.

In practice, the word simulation is used in a variety of related but somewhat different senses. For example, if someone refers to the simulation of an economy, or of some other set of real phenomena, he probably is referring to the combined activity of building a model of that set of phenomena and also of studying and/or using the model by means of the kind of simulation approach defined above. While building a model it is, of course, important to give some thought to its eventual solution and use. However, any particular model might be expressed in any one of various languages and might be solved and used by means of more than one approach. This being the case, it does not seem overly useful for most purposes to classify models either according to the intended techniques of solution alone or even simply according to the language in which they happen to be expressed.[2]

Not only is the term simulation used in different senses, but also a number of other words are used to identify activities or methods which might properly be regarded as specialized uses of a simulation approach. Both gaming and Monte Carlo methods are cases in point. The former may be characterized by the fact that contestants are used as components in models studied by simulation techniques. The

---

[2] Anyone who has read the excellent article [6] by Cohen and Cyert will recognize that this paragraph takes some issue with the manner in which they classify models. Nevertheless, at a more substantive level the author of this paper is in nearly complete agreement with the views they express about the implications of modern computers for model building.

latter may be characterized by the fact that probability models are studied by simulation techniques.

*   *   *

Simulation techniques and studies may be useful in the specification of operating characteristics, in the following ways:

1. Simulation techniques make possible the effective study of models containing large numbers of components, variables and relationships of almost any desired form. They more completely free research workers to be guided by considerations relating to adequacy of representation.

2. Simulation techniques make it feasible to carry out sensitivity analyses on a model. The model can be run many times with the value of one or more parameters being altered between runs. The resulting variations in time paths of endogenous variables can be observed, and related to the corresponding alterations of parameters. After finding out how sensitive these results are to specific differences in the size of parameters, the investigator is in a much better position to decide where to apply additional research effort in parameter estimation.

3. Simulation techniques permit specific implications of models to be determined. By so doing they make it possible to carry out testing at various levels of aggregation, ranging from the level of individual components up to the level of highly aggregative phenomena such as national income. This is extremely important because achievement of more adequate testing is one of the most serious problems facing model builders.

4. Simulation, or closely related Monte Carlo studies, can be useful in supplementing or extending modern multivariate statistical techniques of estimating parameters in operating characteristics. In effect these techniques enable operating characteristics to be fitted to bodies of data by systematic trial-and-error procedures. This may become of greatest importance when dealing with various kinds of nonlinear relationships for which other methods of estimation are either unknown or too costly.

Simulation studies can also be used to improve our knowledge about how existing statistical techniques work in the face of specification errors of various sorts. The very interesting studies of Summers (20) illustrate this type of use.

COMPUTER SIMULATION OF COMPLEX, LARGE-SCALE SYSTEMS

Economic systems are complex organizations involving the behavior of hundreds of millions of complicated decision units and their interaction. Models involving hundreds of millions of components can be conceived of but their construction and use pose problems that appear insuperable both from the standpoint of completely specifying such models and from that of studying and using them if they could be constructed. There are, however, various means by which satisfactory computer simulation of large-scale systems can be made feasible. Many of these are discussed in detail by Orcutt, Greenberger, Korbel and Rivlin (16), but some of the more important means are as follows:

1. *Building-Block Approach.* One rather simple but essential procedure is that of using a building-block approach. Construction of a large-scale model and of a large-scale computer program requires an extended effort over time by many individuals with many skills. Extensive testing of individual pieces must must be carried out before the pieces are assembled, and even after they have been assembled, it frequently may be necessary to modify some pieces. Also in finding and in eliminating the errors in a large and complex computer program it is important to be able to do it piece by piece. And even after it is assembled, it frequently may be desirable to alter a particular operating characteristic, or parameter, or the initial composition of components and their status variables. For these reasons it is highly useful to take the individual components of a model as building blocks and construct them and the over-all model so that they are like the fully plugable components of a modern piece of electronic equipment.

2. *Use of Block-Recursive Models.* Given that a building-block approach is to be used in constructing and simulating a large-scale model on a computer, it is of considerable practical importance that the model be block-recursive, at least in its broad outlines. If it is assumed for purposes of illustration that individual families are treated as blocks, then in order for a model to be block-recursive it is necessary, for example, that a family's expenditures on clothing during a month should not have such an immediate chain of consequences as both to alter income payments to the family and also thereby alter the family's expenditure on clothing during the same

month. This is thus a much less restrictive requirement than that of full recursiveness. Wold makes an impressive case for the use of recursive models (24) and all of Tinbergen's models have this property. Models of Klein, however, must be put in a reduced form before they have this property. Whether or not a real economy can be adequately represented by a block-recursive model depends upon the choice of blocks and how short time lags can be without being represented as zero time lags. Given flexibility in choice of blocks and the use of very short time lags where appropriate, it is difficult to see how the requirement of block-recursiveness places any serious limitations on the model builder. The advantage of working with models which are block-recursive is that digital computers now available all perform their operations in a sequential fashion. This does not prevent solving sets of reasonably small numbers of linear simultaneous equations. It does make extremely difficult or impossible the handling of large numbers of nonlinear simultaneous equations. Use of block-recursive models does limit any given set of simultaneous equations to those needed in generating the output of a single block and thus greatly facilitates computer simulation with computing equipment that is or will be available within the next few years.

3. *Replication of Components.* Given a building-block approach, another major method of facilitating the design and computer simulation of large-scale complex models is to replicate components. This means that while large numbers of components may be used in a model these components are restricted to a relatively small number of major types. Components of the same major type will have identical operating characteristics but may, of course, have different series of values for their status variables and different series of values for their input variables. The advantages of this kind of replication in terms of saving labor in developing and programing a model are obvious and important. There are, however, deeper and more subtle advantages to such replication that relate to estimation and testing of the operating characteristics of the basic components. A full discussion of these is beyond the scope of this paper, but it may be pointed out that replication has essentially the same importance for learning about the behavior and response mechanism of components that it has for experimental design in general.

4. *Treatment of Model as a Probability Sample.* A fourth basic method for achieving effective computer simulation of models that, conceptually at least, involve millions of micro-components, is to re-

gard the components used in computer simulations as probability samples of the components in more extensive conceptual models of economic systems. This can reduce the number of components actually handled in a computer simulation to something less than the hundred thousand or so that are manageable with computers now available. The results obtained from the computer models may then be appropriately blown up in the same way that results obtained by sample surveys are blown up to yield figures appropriate for the populations sampled.

COMPUTER SIMULATION OF A DEMOGRAPHIC MODEL—AN EXAMPLE

As one step in demonstrating the feasibility and potential usefulness of simulation techniques in connection with the development and use of models of economies built in terms of micro-components, Orcutt, Greenberger, Korbel and Rivlin (16) constructed and carried out computer simulations of a demographic model of the United States household sector.

The basic components of the model are individuals and combinations of individuals such as married couples and families. The family units form, grow, diminish and dissolve as married couples have children and get divorced and individuals age, marry and die. These outputs of the basic components in a given month depend on the status variables that characterize each component as of the beginning of the month and on the inputs into each component during the month. The operating characteristics, which serve to relate outputs of components to input and status variables, are stochastic in nature; i.e., it is the probabilities of occurrence of certain outputs rather than the outputs themselves which are regarded as functions of input and status variables. For example, the probability that a woman will give birth to a child during a given month was estimated, on the basis of available data, to depend on a nonlinear, multivariate function of her marital status, age, number of previous births, interval since previous birth or since marriage, month and year. The model is recursive in that the probabilities determined for the possible outputs of each component in any period depend only on previously determined input and status variables.

Solution of the model was achieved by simulation on a large electronic computer. An initial population of over 10,000 individuals was made to be representative of the United States population as of April 1950 by appropriate assignment to these individuals or to groupings of these individuals of sex, race, age, marital status, parity, interval since marriage or previous birth, and family composition. Assignment of these status variables was based on information contained in tabulations of the Bureau of the Census and in various sample surveys carried out by the Survey Research Center of the University of Michigan for the Federal Reserve Board and for a family-planning study by Ronald Freedman, Pascal Whelpton and Arthur Campbell.

The simulations carried out proceeded in one-month steps. Data relating to specific individuals and families were stored on magnetic tape. Operating characteristics, summary information and variables nonspecific to micro-components were stored in high-speed care storage. In each "month" the members of each family were considered in turn. For each possible output of each component a probability of occurrence was specified by use of the relevant operating characteristic and the appropriate status and input variables. Whether the output occurred or not was then determined by a random drawing from this probability distribution. For example, if the probability that a male with a particular initial status will die during the month was calculated to be 0.0002, then, in essence, a random drawing was made from a bag containing two black balls for every 9,998 white balls. The man either died and was eliminated from the population (and from his family) or he lived through the month depending on the outcome of the draw. In practice, however, random numbers generated by the computing machine provided a less cumbersome method of making the random drawings than balls in a bag.

When each possible output for each unit had been considered in this way, the first "pass" or month was complete. The whole procedure was then repeated for the second month and as many more as desired. Each succeeding month was begun with a population of components which was slightly different both in size and composition from the preceding one, since some individuals had died or married, some couples had divorced, some babies had been born and all surviving individuals were one month older.

Several simulation runs covering part or all of the interval from April 1950 to April 1960 were carried out using operating characteristics estimated on the basis of data from available sources. Simulation runs, involving systematic variations in critical operating characteristics, also were carried out.

As each simulation run was carried out the computer was used to summarize the micro-changes taking place and to feed out aggregative monthly information about births, deaths, marriages and divorces. At selected intervals cross-sectional tabulations of the developing populations also were produced by the computer. The aggregative time series and frequency distributions produced in this way were then blown up to provide estimates relating to the real population and where appropriate these estimates were compared with available aggregative data about the United States population and its composition.

The use of simulation techniques by the authors of this demographic study does not, of course, offer any guarantee in itself that they have produced an acceptable and useful population model. However, by producing a feasible means of solution it permitted them to introduce a variety of interactions, variables, nonlinearities and stochastic considerations into their model which they otherwise would have been forced to leave out despite strong evidence of their importance. In addition, by providing a means of solution it made possible comparison of generated results with observed time series and cross sectional data and thus permitted testing of a sort that would not otherwise have been possible.

CONCLUDING REMARKS

A simulation approach to the study and use of models is more easily understood and mastered by nonmathematicians than more conventional mathematical techniques. This aspect of a simulation approach has made it attractive to many research workers and might be expected to have a particular significance for social scientists as well as for business men and government officials.

From the revolution in computing technology of the last one or two decades, the simulation approach has emerged as a practical means of studying and using more nearly realistic models of economic systems. In fact it is the only known approach to the satisfactory study and use of any of the existing dynamic models of economic systems for which any pretense of realism can be claimed. No one can say with certainty that purely deductive mathematical techniques could not be developed to do the required job. However, given the rapid development of survey research techniques and other improved means of data collection about micro-units, and given the rapid development of multivariate statistical techniques of estimating nonlinear relationships, it seems obvious that future models of economic systems will be much less amenable to conventional mathematical analysis than models previously developed. Therefore, a simulation approach to the study and use of models of economic systems has become essential and probably will continue to be so for a long time.

It seems reasonably clear to this author that, during the next decade at least, simulation studies of large complex economic systems will be carried out most effectively on extremely fast digital computers. However, analogue computers have some advantages and some adherents, and the interested reader would benefit by studying the work of Tustin (22).

references

1. I. Adelman and F. Adelman, "The Dynamic Properties of the Klein-Goldberger Model," *Econometrica*, Oct. 1959, *27*, 596-625.
2. A. Aftalion, "La realité des surproductions générales," *Rev. Econ. Pol.*, 1909, pp. 209-10, referred to in A. Hansen, *Business Cycles and National Income*, New York, 1951, p. 356.
3. E. H. Chamberlin, "An Experimental Imperfect Market," *Jour. Pol. Econ.*, Apr. 1948, *56*, 95-108.
4. C. Clark, "A System of Equations Explaining the U. S. Trade Cycle 1921-41," *Econometrica*, Apr. 1949, *17*, 93-124.
5. D. Cochrane and G. Orcutt, "A Sampling Study of the Merits of Autoregressive and Reduced Form Transformations in Regression Analysis," *Jour. Am. Stat. Assoc.*, Sept. 1949, *44*, 356-72.
6. K. Cohen and R. Cyert, *Computer Models in Dynamic Economics*. Carnegie Inst. of Tech. Behavioral Theory of the Firm Working Paper No. 20. Pittsburgh, 1960.
7. J. Duesenberry, O. Eckstein, and G. Fromm, "Stability and Instability in the American Economy," mimeo. paper prepared for Social Science Research Council Conference on Economic Stability, 1958.
8. I. Fisher, *Mathematical Investigations in the Theory of Value and Prices*. New Haven, 1925 (first published in 1892), p. 44, quoted in N. F. Morehouse, R. H. Strotz, and S. J. Horwitz, "An Electro-Analog Method for Investigating Problems in Economic Dynamics: Inventory Oscillations," *Econometrica*, Oct. 1950, *18*, 313-28.
9. L. Klein, "The Use of Econometric Models as a Guide to Economic Policy," *Econometrica*, Apr. 1947, *15*, 111-51.
10. ———, *Economic Fluctuations in the United States 1921-41*, Cowles Commission Monogr. 11. London, 1950.
11. ——— and A. Goldberger, *An Econometric Model of the United States, 1929-1952*. Amsterdam: North Holland Publishing Co., 1955.

12. W. Leontief, *The Structure of the American Economy.* 2nd ed. Cambridge: Harvard University Press, 1951.
13. ———, "Static and Dynamic Theory," *Studies in the Structure of the American Economy.* New York: Oxford University Press, 1953.
14. G. Orcutt, "A Study of the Autoregressive Nature of the Time Series Used for Tinbergen's Model of the Economic System of the United States, 1919-1932," *Jour. Royal Stat. Soc.,* Ser. B, 1948, *10,* 1-53.
15. ——— and S. James, "Testing the Significance of Correlation Between Time Series," *Biometrika,* Dec. 1948, *35,* 397-413.
16. ———, M. Greenberger, J. Korbel, and A. Rivlin, *Microanalysis Of Socioeconomic Systems: A Simulation Study.* New York: Harper & Brothers, Publishers, 1961.
17. M. Shubik, "Bibliography on Simulation, Gaming and Allied Topics," *Jour. Am. Stat. Assoc.,* Dec. 1960, *55.*
18. E. Slutsky, "The Summation of Random Causes as the Source of Cyclic Processes," *Econometrica,* 1937, *5,* 105-46.
19. A. Smithies, "Economic Fluctuations and Growth," *Econometrica,* Jan. 1957, *25,* 1-52.
20. R. Summers, "A Capital-Intensive Approach to the Small-Sample Properties of Various Simultaneous Equation Estimators," abstract in *Econometrica,* Apr. 1959, *27,* 302-3.
21. J. Tinbergen, *Statistical Testing of Business-Cycle Theories.* Geneva: League of Nations, Economic Intelligence Service, 1939.
22. A. Tustin, *The Mechanism of Economic Systems.* Cambridge: Harvard University Press, 1953.
23. K. Wicksell, "Krisernes Gata," *Statsokon Tidsskrift* (1907), 255-86, quoted in R. Frisch, "Propagation Problems and Impulse Problems in Dynamic Economics," *Economic Essays in Honor of Gustav Cassel,* London: G. Allen & Unwin, Ltd., 1933, 171-206.
24. H. Wold, in association with L. Jureen, *Demand Analysis.* New York: John Wiley & Sons, 1953.
25. G. Yule, "Why Do We Sometimes Get Nonsense Correlations Between Time Series?" *Jour. Royal Stat. Soc.,* 1926, *89,* 1-64.

9. the Carnegie Tech management game

K. J. COHEN, R. M. CYERT, W. R. DILL, A. A. KUEHN,
M. H. MILLER, T. A. VAN WORMER, and P. R. WINTERS

Business games, in general, consist of two parts—external environment and internal decisions. The games have usually been built around some given market in which the players making up the several teams are competing. The teams or firms generally are required to make such decisions as setting price, determining output, etc. The environment, which is normally programed on an electronic computer, contains the various functions, such as the demand curve, which determine the outcome for each firm of the decisions made. The firms usually receive some form of income statement and balance sheet, and the outcome of their decisions can be traced in the ebb and flow of the accounts on the financial statements.

Reprinted in part from K. J. Cohen, R. M. Cyert, W. R. Dill, A. A. Kuehn, M. H. Miller, T. A. Van Wormer, and P. R. Winters, "The Carnegie Tech Management Game," *The Journal of Business,* XXXIII (1960), 303-321, with the permission of the authors and the University of Chicago Press.

The research involved in the construction of the game has been supported by grants from the research funds of the Graduate School of Industrial Administration, from special funds provided by the Ford Foundation for the study of organizational behavior and from a grant by the Bankers Trust Company of New York for research in finance.

In addition to the authors, a number of others have participated in varying degrees in the construction of the game. M. L. Anshen has made numerous contributions to the design of the marketing area and to the game as a whole. W. W. Cooper was responsible for much of the stimulation which got the project under way and has given generously of his advice and time throughout the gestation period. D. C. Dearborn assisted in the design of the financial sections of the game, and F. Tonge was codesigner of the production section. A. Federowicz made important contributions to the programing of the game, and E. Evans also aided considerably in the beginning stages of the programing.

The environment is designed to simulate, at least to some degree, the real world. The decisions that must be made by the members of the firms are modeled on the types of decisions actually made in business firms. The level of the decision varies, but most games concentrate on decisions at a high executive level. The development of the computer has stimulated the growth of business games by making it possible to devise environments which are faithful simulations of segments of the economy. As the simulation of the environment becomes more realistic, so also can the decisions that must be made become closer to the decisions of an actual business firm.

It was, in fact, a basic article of faith of the development group of the Carnegie game that if the realism of business games could be increased, a more effective educational and research tool than previously existed would be created. After a period of development and experimental trials we now have a game which we feel has achieved the kind of complexity and realism desired. It is the purpose of this article to explain the game in some detail and then to discuss the education and research possibilities of the game.

I. DESCRIPTION OF THE GAME

The packaged detergent industry has served as a general model for the industry of the game. The selection of this industry for our model was primarily one of convenience. Its advantages included the existence of a national market, a small number of firms, and a set of differentiated products. In addition, some members of the development group had an intimate knowledge of the industry. The game is not, however, an exact simulation of the detergent industry. Only those features deemed useful in terms of the purposes of the game were used.

There are three companies in the game. The players have the role of executives in the three competing companies. Each firm consists of one factory, located in one of the four geographical territories that comprise the total detergent market. At this factory, there are the following facilities: (1) a raw-materials warehouse, (2) production facilities that can be used to produce different mixes of product, (3) a

We should also like to thank the members of the Carnegie Tech faculty, the members of the Ford Seminar at Denver, and the graduate students at Carnegie who served as guinea pigs for the original plays of the game.

factory warehouse for the storage of finished product, and (4) offices and facilities for new-product research and development.

The firm maintains, in addition, a district warehouse for finished products in each of the four regions. These facilities, in contrast with the facilities at the central-plant location, are leased rather than owned.

At the beginning of the game, each firm is "given" one product neither very good nor very bad in terms of its basic characteristics, washing power, sudsing power, and gentleness. By expenditures for new-product research, teams can generate new products. If, on the basis of laboratory reports or market test data, a team wants to put a new product into production, it can do so, as long as the total number of brands in production does not exceed three.

The factory makes all products with the same equipment, using the same work force. In other words, during the month the work force divides its time among products which are scheduled in sequence for production on the same equipment. The team of managers is not concerned, therefore, with detailed scheduling of products among men or machines, and they can regard equipment and work force as homogeneous.

All products in the game are developed from a basic set of seven available raw materials. The team must order raw materials from suppliers in advance of their use in production, but teams can assume that deliveries will be made on schedule. Lead times vary for different materials, and prices will fluctuate seasonally and with general economic conditions. All suppliers of raw materials are assumed to offer a discount of 3 per cent if the team pays its bills within 1 month of delivery of the materials. Payment is required within 2 months of delivery.

Production within each 1-month operating period is scheduled by the players, but the actual monthly output does not necessarily meet their schedule. The computer is programed to impose realistic constraints on the attainment of production goals. Rules in the machine determine how output is affected by raw-material run-outs, by expenditures for maintenance, by limits to plant capacity and to the utilization of overtime, by limits to the rate at which the work force can be expanded, and by undertime and overtime effects on employee productivity. Production costs, as well as output, will be affected by these factors, and costs, in addition, will depend on longer-run decisions of the team to expand capacities for production and for inventory storage.

All production for a given month is presumed available at the warehouse to which it has been consigned at the beginning of the following month. Realistic shipping times and costs are associated with shipments from factory warehouse to district warehouses or from one district warehouse to another. Sales lost because of inventory run-outs over 1 week old cannot be regained, and run-outs carry penalties for future demand.

As sales, the company counts shipments from the factory or district warehouses to its customers who are wholesalers or retail chains. All products which the firm has or can develop are presumed to be distributed at the retail level through supermarkets and grocery stores for use in the home. The firm sets one price for each product in each region, and retail prices may vary considerably by region and by individual store.

In any month, sales for the company depend on the total retail demand for soaps and detergents, which is sharply seasonal, and on the relative effectiveness of the company, vis-à-vis its competitors, in influencing consumer behavior by advertising, by pricing decisions, by outlays for sales force and promotional efforts, and by product characteristics. Consumer response to these variables may vary in the different regions.

To develop new products or to improve existing products, the team must spend money for product research and development. The amount spent determines the probability of generating new-product ideas. As in real life, most new-product ideas will not be worth very much; and even when a good product is developed, its superiority need not be immediately apparent. Laboratory reports on new products will describe the composition (in terms of the seven raw materials), the requirements for them in quantity, their characteristics (washing power, etc.) as revealed by laboratory tests, and the raw material cost per case at current raw-material prices.

If the players think a product idea is worth further study, they can spend money to draw a sample of consumers and to test their product preference. From such test studies, the team will have to decide whether or not to put the product into full-scale production.

Each company is a "going concern" at the beginning of the game. It will have, as noted, a product and a plant to produce the product. The financial condition with which the firm begins the game can be made to vary, depending on the educational objectives of the particular play. Normally, however, we start with each team in reasonably sound financial condition with a modest liquid reserve and an established dividend policy.

The firm can obtain additional funds during play in most of the ways that would be open to a real management group, but they must anticipate their needs for funds. Except for emergency measures, which are described below, the quickest means of financing—a 3-month bank loan—requires a month between the filing of an application and the release of funds to the firm. To qualify for a short-term bank loan, the company must meet specific requirements with respect to liquidity prior to and throughout the life of the loan. The size of loan is limited by the firm's current assets and recent income.

The players can also apply for permission to issue various kinds of marketable debentures. It takes 6 months from the time of application before funds from the issuing of bonds are available, and substantial negotiation and flotation costs are incurred. These forms of financing must be for minimum amounts, and neither can exceed realistic maxima in terms of assets and income. Long-term debt financing also involves realistic restrictive covenants on current ratios, working capital, dividend payments, and sinking funds; but firms can avoid some of these restrictions if they are willing to pay higher coupons.

The players will begin the game with an authorization to issue some additional common stock. If the market value of the stock is adequate, the players may get additional authorization to issue common stock. Funds from new flotations will be available 6 months after the team applies to market the shares at the price then ruling. Flotation costs are substantially higher than in the case of debentures. The market price of the stock of each firm is computed and posted each month. The function, based on recent research findings, makes price vary in the long run according to the growth potential of the industry, to other investment opportunities available to the shareholders in the market, and to the demonstrated efficiency of the players in managing the shareholders' investment. In the short run, price may also vary in response to changes in dividend policy. . . .

If the firm gets into financial difficulties, there will be provisions for temporary relief. The team can sell government bonds to get immediate access to extra cash. Players can delay 1 month, at the cost of their discount, on settling accounts with suppliers. If the firm meets minimal requirements, the due dates for short-term bank loans can be extended.

Plans that the players make for each operating period will be checked by the computer for financial feasibility. If they are not feasible, the players may have to redo the plans and will incur the realistic penalties of improvising, some immediate and some delayed.

The players may wish to expand their plant at one or more points during the game, particularly since there are costs associated with overutilization of facilities. They are permitted to expand production and storehouse facilities at the same localities, but not to add new locations. The capacity of district warehouses may be expanded simply by leasing new space, but the capacity of all other facilities can be expanded only by capital investment. The players may enter into contracts to enlarge the raw-materials warehouse, production plant and equipment, or the factory warehouse. Expenditures for each of these three purposes must be unitary; that is, they cannot specify expenditures for particular kinds of storage space or for particular kinds of equipment. After a period of 6 months, when construction is completed, the costs of production and storage will be adjusted to reflect the additions to capacity. . . .

This, then, summarizes the main characteristics of the companies and of the industry in which they operate. Companies can be differentiated from each other in many ways. Each, of course, will eventually have products with different characteristics. The computer can be programed easily so that they will differ in cost structure, in initial financial position, in plant capacity, in access to markets, or in a variety of other ways.

players' actions

The basic actions of the players must be oriented around two activities. They must analyze the output of the computer, and, on the basis of this analysis, they must make decisions. The output of the computer is detailed and varied and is designed to be complete enough to allow modern mathematical techniques to be utilized. It will be necessary for the firms to develop a system of accounting as well as a system for processing the information received. The magnitude of the problem can be better appreciated by looking at the kind of information received in the areas of production, marketing, and finance. Production men will receive forms that summarize the following:

1. The raw-materials situation: stocks on hand, quantities on order, deliveries during past month, usage during past month, and current prices
2. Factory performance: actual quantities produced and shipped (by product and destination), raw-material and labor usage by product, employment levels, amount of overtime, maintenance expenditures, equipment downtime
3. Warehouse transactions: opening and closing inventories, receipts from other warehouses, shipments to other warehouses, sales, and receipts from factory

The production men will also get, at the beginning of the game and later at irregular intervals, information about the following:

1. Raw-material requirements for each product
2. Required lead times for raw-material orders
3. Space requirements for raw-materials storage
4. Estimates of "normal" worker productivity for each product
5. Current hiring and firing costs
6. Current wage rates (straight time and overtime)
7. Space requirements for storing finished goods
8. Charges for excess inventory storage
9. Shipping costs and required shipping times from factory to warehouses
10. Storage costs at district warehouses
11. Price changes for various raw materials

They will get less explicit "reports of past experience" about plant capacity, about the impact of maintenance expenditures, raw-material shortages, overtime, and undertime on production, and about the rules for rescheduling shipments to warehouses if actual production differs from scheduled production.

The marketing men will know, after each operating period, the following information about their firms:

1. Expenditures by product and by region for advertising and for sales force and promotional efforts and total expenditures for market research, sales office and administration, and product research and development
2. Information about the environment, such as current and forecasted annual rates of gross national product, salesmen's reports on brands introduced and dropped by competitors in each region
3. Sales by brand and by district warehouse

In proportion to specific expenditures on market research, they will receive estimates of what competitors have spent on advertising and research activity and free predictions of approximately the usual reliability on gross national product for the coming 5 years. As the occasion warrants, they will receive laboratory reports on new products. These reports will scale the product on sudsing, washing power, and gentleness. They will tell raw-material requirements and raw-material and production costs. There will also be estimates of expected productivity in making the new product.

The company can pay to get additional marketing data on brand preferences of consumers and on market variables, such as share of market, or competitors' advertising, distribution, and prices to wholesalers.

Initially, the marketing men will start with some specific data about such things as (1) the costs of market studies on various scales and (2) the characteristics of the company's given products (and, to a lesser extent, of competitors' products).

They will have less explicit "experiential" data on the potential gains from different kinds of marketing and research expenditures, about the structure of the market, and about the firm's position vis-à-vis competitors.

The finance men will receive at the end of each month the following kinds of information:

1. A balance sheet, with special reports on inventory position, plant and equipment accounts, construction obligations outstanding, and status of loans and securities outstanding
2. Summary of receipts and disbursement during the month
3. Statement of financial commitments for next and future months
4. Current information on the availability of financing
5. General information on money and capital markets
6. An income statement, with special reports on cost of goods sold and cost of materials used
7. At the end of every quarter a balance sheet and an income statement for each competitor issued to each firm

As the occasion warrants, they will receive notice of violations of loan covenants.

In addition, they will have detailed initial reports on the way in which accounts are kept and on the way in which various cash receipts and disbursements do—or can—occur. The conditions under which they can obtain various forms of financing will be spelled out in detail, along with explanations of the length of time before funds become available, of the conditions for extending a loan, and of the penalties for failing to meet commitments.

This information then becomes the basis for a whole complex of decisions. In the area of production, the players must regularly

1. Order raw materials
2. Decide on size of labor force
3. Decide how much overtime to authorize
4. Plan how much to spend for maintenance of plant and equipment
5. Schedule the total quantity of production for the month by product
6. Decide how to allocate production among warehouses
7. Decide what transshipments of existing inventories need to be made from factory to district warehouses or among district warehouses

In the marketing area, the players must regularly

1. Set prices by product and by region
2. Determine advertising expenditures by product and by region
3. Decide distribution expenditures (for sales force and promotion) by product and by region

In the financial area, the players must regularly

1. Estimate net cash requirements for operations in the coming month
2. Authorize total receipts and disbursements for the coming month
3. Arrange for payments of funds for taxes, for interest, for construction, for retirement of debt, and for purchase of government bonds
4. Decide what share of profits should be allocated as dividends to stockholders
5. Decide (in the case of inadequate cash reserves) what steps should be taken to cut expenditures

Most of these decisions bind the company only in the short run. The decisions on dividend payments need be made only quarterly, and some of the others might also be, but most will need to be reviewed and remade every month. These are the decisions which the computer must have in satisfactory form before it can produce operating results for the next period.

In addition, to survive and grow in the face of competition from one or more other firms, the players must be prepared to consider at frequent intervals the following:

1. Expenditures for research on new products and for test market studies on consumer acceptance of the products
2. Expenditures for general market research into the nature of con-

sumer preferences, into the patterns of retail sales, or into the performances of competitors

3. The desirability of dropping, changing, or adding products or of extending marketing efforts into a new territory
4. Investment in new facilities for the storage of raw materials or finished goods
5. Investment in new plant and equipment for production
6. The advisability of applying for
    a) Renegotiation of current debt
    b) Additions to working capital by short-term bank loans
    c) Long-term additions to capital by issuing stock or by selling bonds

Decisions on these matters may not be made very often, and, when made, they will frequently take the nature of long-term commitments. But the players must be continually alert to their long-run interests and must anticipate their requirements while they still have time to act. Specific instructions about how much to spend or about what to do must be fed to the computer.

In developing the Carnegie game, we had as our objective a game that would be useful both as a teaching device and as a research tool. In the next two sections we shall discuss the potential of the game as we see it in each of these directions.

II. USES OF THE GAME IN EDUCATION

Our educational objectives in designing the Carnegie Tech management game were more ambitious than the goals of designers of the simpler games. Ben R. Faden has said that the educational purpose of the IBM game is "to help us to discard emotional blocks and to use our best judgment."[1] In a similar vein, an executive writes of his experience with the AMA games:

> The complex problems of running a business are presented in such a way that seems to facilitate rapid comprehension, active participation, and intense involvement in the process of planning, review, and analysis.[2]

The emphasis is not on teaching managers specific skills; it is limited to reminding experienced specialists that the functions—and people—

---

[1] From the *Proceedings of the National Symposium on Management Games, University of Kansas, May, 1959,* pp. iv-11.

[2] Clifford Craft, "Competitive Management Simulation," *Journal of Industrial Engineering,* September-October, 1959, p. 363.

of a business are interdependent and that many decisions must be made under time pressure by the co-operative judgments of several individuals.[3]

The undergraduate or graduate student of business (or sometimes even the seasoned executive), though, does not become a manager simply by discarding emotional blocks or participating intensely in an absorbing, but grossly oversimplified, substitute for a real management environment. We began work on the Carnegie Tech game with the hope of doing more—of developing an environment in which players could test and develop some of the positive skills which a manager must employ. This concern is reflected both in the design of the game and in the arrangements we have adopted for its administration.

What must a manager do well to be effective? We do not pretend, of course, to have anything like the whole answer to this, but we believe that the following skills, at least, will be universally recognized as important.

1. *An ability to abstract, organize, and use information from a complex and diffuse environment.* Managers live in a world which lavishes information on them but which affords them little time and little guidance about how to use it. A key function of management is to discover the pertinence of various data to the organization's objectives, to isolate the problems which deserve immediate attention, and to identify the constraints which must be observed in seeking a solution.

The way in which the game is currently being administered seems also to add to its utility as an environment for sharpening information-processing skills. Two features of the administrative arrangements are particularly important—team size and the subordination of each team to a board of directors.

The Carnegie Tech game is complex enough to permit ten-man teams whose members have clearly differentiated functions to perform. Because no one man consistently has time to absorb the information made available to the team, players must learn to interpret and summarize incoming results in a way that helps their teammates

---

[3] We are speaking here of the simpler "general management" games which have received most of the attention and publicity in the last year or two. There are a number of games—some which James Lubin at the University of Pennsylvania has developed, for example—whose purpose is more didactic: to persuade clerks of the superiority of a new method of production scheduling or to demonstrate the efficacy of modern inventory-control techniques.

as well as themselves. The financial officers must be able to talk to the production officers about relevant aspects of the company's financial condition without discussing all the details of cost trends, current cash position, stock prices, or negotiations with outside lenders. The marketing officers must be able to translate their detailed marketing experience into a sales forecast on which the finance officers can base their cash budgets and projected income statements and on which the production officers can base orders for raw materials, production schedules, and schedules for shipment of finished goods to district warehouses.

In the first extended play of the game, boards of three to four faculty members were appointed for each firm. The director's job was essentially to test the players' understanding of their environment, to force them to communicate information about their positions and plans, and to direct their attention—when appropriate—to particular problems and goals. Regular meetings of the boards of directors with the members of their firms were held at the end of every (simulated) quarter or half-year of play. At these meetings the officers of the firms had to review the results of their past operations and to present their plans for future operations.

At the end of every (simulated) year of play, each firm was required to present a written annual report to their stockholders. This report had to include financial statements for the current and recent years; a review of developments in production, sales, finance, new products, plant facilities, and organization during the current year; an evaluation of the present competitive position of the firm; and a review of plans for changes in operations and for new investments in products, market development, and new-plant or warehouse facilities for the future, with an explanation of the reasons behind these plans.

2. *An ability to forecast and to plan.* The complexity of modern business operations and the time lags that occur before the effects of decisions are realized put a premium on the manager's ability to look ahead. The student of management needs to recognize at an early stage not only the immediate, but the cumulative, effects of his actions (or lack of action). He should also practice forecasting consequences of his decisions so that he can measure what he accomplishes against what he planned to achieve.

Over and above the presence of directors and of time pressure on the officers, though, the game itself is designed to encourage planning and to penalize lack of attention to future needs. The finance officers, for example, must make sure that sufficient funds are available to carry out the planned operating decisions and to pay the firm's debts when due, developing and applying to that end techniques of cash-flow forecasting and cash budgeting. If the funds available in any period are not sufficient to meet the firm's immediate financial obligations and to carry out its currently programed operating decisions, the machine will reject the move. The team will then have to improvise a new program consistent with its resources, a process which will involve costs, some immediate and visible, such as loss of discounts, and some subtle and delayed, such as loss of continuity in programs whose results depend on the cumulated level of expenditures.

3. *An ability to combine the role of generalist and specialist.* The image which simple management games present of managers as a team of generalists, all concerned with over-all company policy, seems to have a limited basis in real life. Most managers, as individuals, are as much specialists as generalists. Even in the top positions of organizations, men are committed by experience, expertise, loyalties and job responsibilities to subareas like production, marketing and finance. Their commitments as specialists affect their behavior on top policy decisions; and, at the same time, their identification with the enterprise as a whole requires them to co-operate at lower levels in the planning of many detailed operating decisions.

More than the simpler games, the Carnegie Tech game may lure the careless player into the trap of excessive specialization. But in real life, too, the manager must learn to be a generalist under conditions where the temptations are strong to remain a specialist. Here we rely primarily on the unsatisfactory income statements and balance sheets of teams which do not plan and co-ordinate their activities to draw their attention to the needs for considering the firm as a whole. The boards of directors can also be expected to comment on the lack of integration in what various groups from the firm are doing. Through these devices we have tried to emphasize interdepartmental co-operation both on short-term actions and on broad policy questions.

4. *An ability to work effectively with other people.* Managers must effectively maintain three kinds of co-operative working relationships with other people in an organizational setting. In relation to their own superiors—who may be other managers, directors, stockholders, or others who have influence on company goals and on the evaluation of managerial performance—managers are required to negotiate about

the objectives toward which they are working and about the impact of these objectives for decisions about operating the company. Second, when goals have been established or inferred, managers must work together to produce good decisions with the resources that they have at their disposal. Third, managers must work through a subordinate organization to elaborate and implement their policies and decisions.

Our objective in designing the Carnegie Tech management game was to provide an environment in which these abilities might be developed. We do not expect that a game, any more than any other single teaching technique, can take over the whole task of molding men into managers; but we expect that complex management games will earn an important role in such efforts.

* * *

III. ROLE OF THE GAME IN RESEARCH

One of the deficiencies of the current understanding of business games is the lack of appreciation of the research potential of games. During the development of the Carnegie game, on the other hand, one of the key objectives was the research potential of the game. The game has not been in existence long enough to have been utilized extensively for research. Nevertheless, it is possible to see at least five areas—economics, organization, finance, marketing and production—where there are interesting research problems. To demonstrate the method by which the game can be used in research, some of the problems in each area will be examined.

economics

The usefulness of the game for research in economics lies primarily in the study of oligopoly. The two areas for which the game seems most suitable are the analysis of the effects of varying amounts of information about competitors' behavior and the empirical study of decision-making.

Information can be given with varying degrees of uncertainty on competitors' prices, outputs, advertising, investment and research. It would be of interest to attempt to determine the amount of information, both quantity and quality (probability of being accurate), necessary to induce implicit collusion in the market. A similar problem, though one with more measurement difficulties, would be to determine whether or not a kink in the demand curve appears in the minds of the decision-makers as a reduction in the amount of information on competitors is made.

In the empirical study of decision-making a wide variety of questions might be examined. Does full-cost pricing make an appearance? What determines the amount of the markup and changes in the markup? How is output set if marginal calculations are not used? What is the planning horizon of the firms, and what effect does the length of the horizon have on pricing and the internal allocation of resources among advertising, investment and research activities? A large number of such questions, the answers to which could help economists significantly in understanding firm behavior, can be studied empirically by use of the game. At the same time, the decisions involved in such questions are difficult and expensive to study in actual firms.

organization theory

The Carnegie game permits a great deal of experimentation with the way teams of players are organized. Here we can only summarize the arrangements that we plan to try initially and some of the variations we should like to explore.

1. *Team size.* Teams can include anywhere from three to ten men. For educational purposes, we tend toward the larger teams, so that players will have to devote some effort to planning division of labor, to establishing communications and to maintaining organizational stability without sacrificing flexibility.

Eventually we plan to study the effects of variance in team size on performance, on team morale, and on teams' adaptability to change. Thorndike, Shaw and Taylor[4] have raised questions about the effectiveness of group versus individual efforts; Taylor and Bales and Borgatta have raised questions about the "optimal" size of work groups.[5]

---

[4] R. L. Thorndike, "On What Type of Task Will a Group Do Well?" *Journal of Abnormal and Social Psychology,* XXXIII (1938), 409-13; M. E. Shaw, "A Comparison of Individuals and Small Groups in the Rational Solution of Complex Problems," *American Journal of Psychology,* XLIV (1932), 491-504; D. W. Taylor, P. C. Berry, and C. H. Block, "Does Group Participation when Using Brainstorming Facilitate or Inhibit Creative Thinking?" *Administrative Science Quarterly,* III (1958), 23-47.

[5] D. W. Taylor and W. L. Faust, "Twenty Questions: Efficiency in Problem Solving as a Function of Size of Group," *Journal of Experimental Psychology,*

With the type of task that the game imposes, we shall want to ask whether the effects of increasing group size are continuous. Limits to the way in which the task can be subdivided may, for example, make a team of six men better than a team of five or seven.

Initially, team membership will be fixed at the start of the game. As another variation, it would be useful to give the job of running a company in the game to one or two men and let them build their own team. The process by which they create new jobs and select men to fill them may at least tell us something about the generality of Parkinson's law.

2. *Team structure.* By its complexity, the Carnegie game is the first game in which the task itself might strongly encourage players to adopt hierarchical patterns of organization. We can further influence the likelihood that hierarchical structures will evolve by (*a*) decisions concerning team size; (*b*) initial assignments of access to information, channels of communication, and responsibility for decisions; (*c*) attention to real-life status differentiations and special skills of the players; (*d*) combinations of experienced and inexperienced players on the same team; and (*e*) modifying the game to complicate and separate still further the marketing, production and finance functions.

Is hierarchical organization inevitable? Guetzkow and Simon[6] present evidence that hierarchical patterns tend to be chosen over nonhierarchical patterns that are theoretically as efficient or more efficient. Does the pattern of organization matter? Guetzkow and Bowes report a simpler production-selling simulation in which organization structure and task performance were not related.[7]

3. *Time per move.* It seems reasonable from early runs to allow 2-3 hours for each move. What happens if the pace is increased? Will we get, as March and Simon anticipate, a neglect of planning and a regression to stopgap, crisis-oriented patterns of behavior? To what extent can we cancel the harmful effects of time pressure by the kinds of players we select or by the kinds of organizational patterns that

---

XLIV (1952), 360-68; R. F. Bales and E. F. Borgatta, "Size of Group as a Factor in the Interaction Profile," in P. Hare *et al., Small Groups* (New York: Alfred A. Knopf, 1955), pp. 396-413.

[6] H. Guetzkow and H. A. Simon, "The Impact of Certain Communication Nets upon Organization and Performance in Task-oriented Groups," *Management Science,* I (1955), 233-50.

[7] H. Guetzkow and A. Bowes, "The Development of Organizations in a Laboratory," *Management Science,* III (1957), 380-402.

we impose? Do severe time pressures at an early stage in the life of a team lead to more or to less effective long-run performance?

4. *Spacing of moves.* Where the game is used as part of a training program, some consideration needs to be given to the spacing of moves and to the proper balance between actual play and feedback sessions or other kinds of training activity. This is usually an easy question to answer on the basis of obvious institutional contraints, but the literature on human learning suggests that the spacing of moves can have critical effects on the speed and quality of players' learning.[8]

5. *Information flows.* In later versions of the game, particularly as we study the ways in which player organizations develop and function, we may want to exert more controls on the information that they receive. An important element of the game already is the extent to which players must make decisions about the amounts of information they want to purchase in addition to that which is routinely provided to them. Later we can complicate the task further by restricting amounts and kinds of information that different players receive, by increasing the amount of redundant and irrelevant information that is made available, and by modifying the computer program to increase the amounts of uncertain or contradictory information that are transmitted.

6. *Stability of team membership.* Social scientists have begun to study the impact that the introduction of new members has on organizations. The Carnegie game would provide a more complex environment than has previously been used to replicate and elaborate these studies. The relations between patterns of managerial succession and turnover and such things as organizational stability, intraorganizational conflict, and task performance are important to know about and deserve more attention than they have thus far received.

Many other organizational aspects of the Carnegie game could be mentioned here. In particular, we could elaborate ways in which the game provides an environment for research on organizational processes that promises a combination of the advantages of laboratory experimentation and those of field observation of business firms. There is a wide variety of hypotheses from both areas that can fruit-

---

[8] Currently, the game is being played at the speed of one move a week by men who are taking a full load of regular graduate courses. We do not expect that the Carnegie game can be played effectively in an intensive 1- or 2-day session as many of the simpler games have been played.

fully be explored and tested in the Carnegie game situation. We are confident that the kinds of developments that such gaming models permit can lead not only to increased empirical understanding of how organizations function but also to better formulations of hypotheses and theories. To the extent that improved versions of the Carnegie game really approach realistic simulation of the operations of particular kinds of industries, they will become important tools for experimenting with different kinds of managerial policies.

finance

It was the hope of those primarily responsible for the design of the finance section that the game might also be useful for the investigation of certain unsolved problems in the finance area that are extremely difficult to attack by conventional methods. It is possible, for example, to run a simulated stock market in conjunction with the game. Because, in our game, the teams can pay dividends and float new shares, the simulation may be rich enough that the technique of direct observation and interview of investors over a considerable period of time—a technique which is far too costly to attempt on an adequate scale in the enormous real-world capital market—may be brought to bear on the problem of how investors actually change valuations in response to, say, changes in the earnings and dividends of the companies in which they are interested.[9]

At the level of the firm, interviews and observation over a long period may help to throw some new light on the role of financial constraints. Is it true, for example, as some have suggested, that finance is essentially passive, i.e., that firms first determine a basic operating and growth strategy and then simply leave to the finance department the task of seeing that the funds are somehow obtained to meet these predetermined goals? Or does finance exert an independent role in the sense that the operating strategy is tailored to fit predetermined financial objectives and self-imposed constraints? Or, assuming that both kinds of behavior are observed on different teams and at different times, are the differences merely matters of personality, or can they be related systematically to objective differences in the economic context in which the decisions were made?

---

[9] One by-product of the process of construction of the game has been that it has pointed up clearly the deficiencies in the existing state of knowledge and provided an additional stimulus to empirical and theoretical research on the determinants of stock prices.

marketing

The research prospects within the marketing sphere of the Carnegie game are much greater than in earlier business games. The Carnegie game is the first to give definition to the marketing situation. This has made it possible to simulate the business environment and market mechanisms more faithfully. Selling packaged detergents and soaps is not the same as selling machine tools, automobiles, clothing, or even food products distributed, in part, through identical retail outlets. An attempt is made in the Carnegie game to provide the marketing manager with the types of data and alternatives that are available in the comparable business setting.

The Carnegie game is scheduled to play an important role in the Graduate School's program of research in marketing. The model used to generate market data creates a laboratory setting for the evaluation of analytical techniques in the interpretation of market statistics. It should prove to be relatively easy to evaluate the usefulness of analytical tools in assisting the players to understand the market situation. Research findings developed in the game environment can be used as a framework for subsequent field research in marketing practice. The better the simulation of the marketing function within the game, the more likely that the findings developed at that level will prove applicable to business practice. As more is learned about market behavior and the mechanisms underlying it, the game can be improved; an improved model of the marketing function would, in turn, set the stage for another round of testing and development.

production

The production section has, perhaps, less potential research use than some of the other areas discussed. The reason is that it was necessary to abstract from the details of the actual factory in order to have a manageable game. Thus production scheduling—a problem on which much attention is being concentrated currently—has been eliminated from the game.

However, there is one big problem still remaining in the production area within the game, and that is the problem of inventory control. The game is an ideal device for testing the effectiveness of a number of proposed inventory-control systems under a variety of sales patterns. As the game progresses and the firms handle three products, the environment becomes complex enough to test any control system. In

addition, the problem of deciding on optimum product mix is present.
A second kind of problem which has not been generally studied by
production men is the question of when to expand productive capacity. Some insight into the empirical aspects of decision-making can
be gained, but, in addition, the game may be an excellent vehicle for
a normative approach to the problem.

conclusion

In all the research and experimental work that is suggested here,
one is, of course, faced with the traditional problem of any all-
laboratory science. The results that one gleans from an experimental
situation cannot necessarily be applied to the world. One cannot
immediately conclude that what follows in the experimental situation
will obviously hold in the real world. This is a problem which has, of
course, faced experimentalists for a long time. There is no particularly
easy way out of this in the game, so that, at a minimum, the results
that are determined from experimentation with the game become
interesting hypotheses about the world, and the researcher is left with
the problem of determining how to test these propositions in the
world.

However, it may be possible, in some areas at least, to determine
the conditions of the game in such a way that one has a stronger
presumption of their applicability in the world. For example, it may
be possible to determine, by having established business executives
play the game, whether or not the same decision-making processes
that they use in business are also applied in the game. It may be
possible, through some of the studies that have been made at Carnegie
Tech of the decision-making processes in business, to categorize the
characteristics of decision-making behavior in the real world and
then, through a study of the individual participants within the firms,
to decide whether or not these same characteristics are being followed
in the behavior of the individuals in the game.

10. in-basket tests and factors in administrative performance

NORMAN FREDERIKSEN,
Research Division, Educational Testing Service

The purpose of the study which I will describe . . . was to learn more about performance in educational administration. There is a tendency, in evaluating administrators, to think in terms of one over-all dimension of goodness or badness. We felt that formulating the evaluation problem in terms of one variable was too simple. One of our purposes was to try to identify some major dimensions of administrative behavior; another was to discover how such dimensions might be related to a variety of other measurable characteristics of people.

The study was a co-operative one, done by staff members of Teachers College, Columbia University, and Educational Testing Service: Dr. Daniel Griffiths of Teachers College, Director of the Project; Dr. John K. Hemphill of ETS, Associate Director; Dr. Glen Stice, Research Associate at ETS, and myself. The study was supported by a grant to Teachers College from the Cooperative Research Program of the U. S. Office of Education.

One difficulty encountered when one tries to study behavior on the job is that it is impossible to tell whether variation in performance should be attributed to differences among the subjects or to differences among the jobs. In this study we eliminated the job as a source of variation by simulating a school and community and giving each one of the 232 subjects the job of being principal of the same simu-

Reprinted from Norman Frederiksen, "In-Basket Tests and Factors in Administrative Performance," *Invitational Conference on Testing Problems, Proceedings* (October 1960), pp. 21-37, with the permission of the author and the Educational Testing Service.

lated school. Enough information about this school and community was provided that subjects could reasonably be expected to take action on the administrative problems presented to them.

The subjects of the investigation were 232 elementary school principals. They came from school districts all over the United States, and they constituted quite a varied group in terms of age, experience and ability.

The test is a fairly elaborate one, requiring five days to administer. About 20 people were tested at one time. The test began on Monday morning, when the examinees were introduced to the school of which each was to be the new principal. The simulated school is Whitman School, located in Jefferson in the hypothetical state of Lafayette. Each subject was temporarily given a new name, Marion Smith. The subjects were instructed that they were not to play a role, that each was to bring to the new job his own background of experience, his own knowledge and personality. During the test he was to perform the duties of the new principal of Whitman School.

The participants spent the first day and a half in learning about Whitman School and its community. First, a film strip was presented which gave the participants an over-all view of Jefferson. Then the principals were given an opportunity to study the Jefferson School-Community Survey which had recently been completed by the School of Education at Lafayette State. Next the group viewed a sound color film which took the subjects inside Whitman, where they saw the faculty and children at work. The subjects were given personnel folders for the teachers and staff, a floor plan of the school, and a staff roster. Study guides were provided to direct the subjects' study of the materials.

On Tuesday morning the indoctrination was continued with additional material for study, including a Staff Handbook, the School Board Handbook, excerpts from the Lafayette school law, copies of the most recent school census, a class size list, the school calendar, and a report of achievement test scores. All this printed material became the principals' files throughout the week. The examinees also listened to tape recordings of school board meetings and conversations involving teachers and parents.

At the end of the day and a half of orientation, the subjects had as much information as would be expected of a new principal in an actual situation. It was now reasonable to expect the subjects to take action on problems arising in the administration of the school.

The balance of the week was devoted to work sessions in which each Marion Smith performed the duties of the principal of Whitman School. All the participants were presented with the same set of administrative problems under the same conditions. Each new principal was given memo pads, letterheads, paper, pencils, and paper clips. He was instructed merely to be the principal. He was not to say what he *would* do—he was to *do* it. He actually wrote memos, called meetings, prepared agendas, made notes in preparation for interviews, and the like.

The primary method of presenting problems in our study was the in-basket test. Such a test consists of facsimiles of the letters, memoranda, and other contents of the in-basket such as is found on every administrator's desk. Four in-basket tests were presented, each requiring a half-day session. About thirty-two problems were included in each in-basket; they were chosen in the light of a theoretical formulation of the job of an elementary school principal.

In addition to the desk work involved in the four in-baskets, the subjects were required to participate in committee work, observe the work of teachers shown in kinescopes, and react to conference situations presented by means of tape recordings.

This is a very brief description of a rather elaborate situational test. The participants tell us that the situation was realistic and that they built up vivid images of the people involved. Each participant received the same opportunities to learn the background, and each was presented with the same problems under identical conditions. Therefore we can attribute differences in behavior to the participants rather than to variations among jobs.

Each principal left an envelope full of memos, letters, reminders, instructions to his secretary, appointment calendars, and the like. How can this material be scored?

The first step towards developing a scoring procedure was to examine in-basket responses to see how respondents differ. As a result of such examination by a number of observers, a large pack of cards was collected, each card containing a statement of some kind of difference observed in the way the principals behaved. The cards contained phrases like "compulsive," "postpones decisions," and "makes unwarranted assumptions." A second source of ideas for scoring categories came from theories of administration and leadership, especially the theories of the Director and Associate Director of the project.

Eventually all these modes of behavior were collapsed to make the

68 scoring categories shown in Table 1. A scoring manual was written which gives appropriate definitions and rules for scoring. Each in-basket problem can be thought of as an opportunity to display the behavior described by the category. On the score sheet a *one* or a *zero* was recorded under each category heading, for each problem, to indicate whether or not the behavior did occur. A total of 132 problems was scored for each of the 68 categories.

The in-baskets were scored by eight scorers, each one scoring a different half in-basket. Reliability was determined by correlating the scores obtained from the odd-item scorers with the scores for the even-item scorers, and correcting for length. Thus the reliabilities reflect both scoring accuracy and amount of consistency in the principals' behavior. The reliabilities which resulted varied from zero to .97, as shown in Table 1.

The 40 categories which are double-starred in Table 1 were chosen for use in the next phase of the analysis. These categories had reliabilities of .52 or higher and a median reliability of .78. The intercorrelations of these 40 scores were computed, and the matrix of intercorrelations was factored. Eight factors were retained; they account for almost all of the common variance among the scores. Rotations were made graphically to produce an oblique factor matrix with simple structure. Table 2 presents the category scores having loadings of .25 or more on each of the factors.

Factor A is called *Exchanging Information*. This interpretation seems quite clear on the basis of the four scores with the highest loadings.

Factor B we call *Discussing Before Acting*. Again the interpretation is clear from the scores with the highest loadings. The "new structure" in *initiates a new structure* is likely to be a committee or other discussion group; the "procedure" in *arrives at a procedure for deciding* is likely to be a discussion.

Factor C might appear to involve precipitate and aggressive action from the categories *concluding decision* and *terminal action*. But the two *following leads* categories also have high loadings. The actions and decisions are thus likely to be made in compliance with suggestions; hence the name *Complying with Suggestions Made by Others*.

Factor D has very high loadings on two categories. The factor is called *Analyzing the Situation* because it appears to involve broad situational analysis of in-basket problems.

Factor E has loadings on categories which imply concern about

Table 1

Reliability of in-Basket Category Scores

Category	Reliability	Category	Reliability
**Estimated Number of Words Written	.94	**Work Scheduled for Same or Next Week	.83
**Number of Items Not Attempted	.97	**Work Scheduled—No Time Specified	.83
**Number of Courses of Action (Usual)	.92	**Leading Action	.90
Rejection of Test Conditions	.59	**Terminal Action	.86
**Number of Subordinates Involved as Individuals	.84	**Follows Lead by Subordinates	.77
**Number of Subordinate Groups Involved	.69	**Follows Lead by Superiors	.71
**Number of Superiors Involved	.60	**Follows Lead by Outsiders	.61
**Number of Outsiders Involved as Individuals	.73	**Follows Pre-Established Structure	.67
Number of Outside Groups Involved	.44	Coordination	.41
**Unusual Action	.52	**Initiates a New Structure	.78
Recognizes Good Work	.71	Delegates Completely	.31
**Aware of Poor Work	.65	Delegates Partially with Control	.24
**Carelessness or Minor Error	.69	Delegates Partially without Control	.59
Socially Insensitive	.38	**Gives Directions or Suggestions	.83
**Relates to Background Material or Other Items	.75	Refers to Superiors	.17
**Conceptual Analysis	.70	**Communicates Face-to-Face	.86
Prejudges, Unwarranted Assumptions, Inappropriate	.35	**Communicates by Telephone	.74
Uses Human Values	.43	**Communicates by Writing	.90
Uses Physical Values	*	**Gives Information to Subordinates	.66
**Uses Program Values	.65	Gives Information to Superiors	.24
**Discusses with Subordinates	.84	**Gives Information to Outsiders	.58
Discusses with Other Principals	.39	Explains Actions to Subordinates	.53
**Discusses with Superiors or Outsiders	.58	Explains Actions to Superiors	.19
**Asks Subordinates for Information or Opinion	.81	Explains Actions to Outsiders	.18
Asks Superiors for Information or Opinion	.41	**Courtesy to Subordinates	.91
Asks Outsiders for Information or Opinion	.46	Courtesy to Superiors	.53
**Requires Further Information for Deciding	.68	**Courtesy to Outsiders	.55
**Delays, Postpones, or Temporizes	.81	**Informality to Subordinates	.92
**Arrives at a Procedure for Deciding	.80	Informality to Superiors	.64
Contingent Decision	.38	Informality to Outsiders	.00
**Concluding Decision	.78	Backs up Staff	.06
**Tentative or Definite Plans Only	.92	Improves Staff	*
**Work Scheduled for Same or Next Day	.77	Improves Working Conditions	*
		Sets a Deadline	.36
		Follow-up or Feedback Planned	.01

*Reliability estimates were not computed because of the extremely low frequency of these scores.

**These items were used in the first factor analysis.

superiors and outsiders, and the negative loading on *delays* implies prompt action. We call this factor *Maintaining Organizational Relationships.*

Factor F is *Organizing Work,* and it is characterized particularly by care in specifying in advance quite exactly when one's work is to be done.

Factor G is called *Responding to Outsiders* because the four categories with the highest loadings all have to do with people outside the organization. We might think of this factor as reflecting concern about community relations.

Factor H is interpreted as *Directing the Work of Others.* Giving directions to subordinates is likely to be done in writing rather than orally, and courtesy is often used, apparently to soften the blow.

A second-order factor analysis revealed two factors which we call X and Y. The saturations of the individual scoring categories were determined, and those saturations of category scores which are .50 or higher are shown in Table 3.

Factor X has high saturations on a number of scores having to do with productivity—number of words written, number of courses of action taken, number of people involved, and so on. There are negative loadings on such categories as *delays or postpones* and *plans only.* We call this second-order factor *Amount of Work Done in Handling Items.*

Factor Y is a bipolar factor with negative loadings on *concluding decisions* and *terminal action* and positive loadings on a variety of scores having to do with deciding how to proceed, getting informed, and having discussions. Hence the name, *Preparation for Decision vs. Taking Final Action.*

The Factor Y loadings shown in Table 3 represent the extremes of a continuum which has a rather marked similarity to certain theories of decision-making. Table 4 identifies six theoretical stages in the process of decision-making. In the parallel columns are shown some selected category scores and their loadings on Factor Y. The agreement between the theoretical formulation and the empirical findings is rather striking. This is, of course, no verification of the theory that one goes through these stages in reaching a decision. There is clear indication, however, that a principal's characteristic behavior in response to a standard set of administrative problems can be described in terms of his position on the continuum of decision development.

A large number of other variables—ratings, inventory scores,

Table 2

Factor Loadings

Factor A: Exchanging Information	**Number of subordinate groups involved** .26
Asks subordinates for information, opinion or advice .50	**Factor D: Analyzing the Situation**
Gives information to subordinates .45	Uses program values .82
Requires further information for deciding .34	Conceptual analysis .75
Gives information to outsiders .31	Aware of poor work .28
Number of subordinate groups involved .29	**Factor E: Maintaining Organizational Relationships**
Number of usual courses of action .25	Number of superiors involved .54
Factor B: Discussing Before Acting	Discusses with superiors or outsiders .42
Work scheduled—time unspecified .63	Number of outsiders involved .41
Discusses with subordinates .62	Relates to background materials or other items .37
Communicates face-to-face .60	Follows lead by outsiders .26
Initiates a new structure .48	Communicates by telephone .26
Arrives at a procedure for deciding .46	Delays, postpones −.38
Tentative or definite plans only .40	**Factor F: Organizing Work**
Number of items attempted .40	Work scheduled for same or next week −.51
Discusses with superiors or outsiders .39	Work scheduled for same or next day .50
Number of usual courses of action .36	Follows pre-established procedure .30
Requires further information for deciding .31	Relates to background information or other items .25
Number of subordinate groups involved .29	Work scheduled—time unspecified −.48
Follows lead by subordinates .29	**Factor G: Responding to Outsiders**
Follows lead by superiors .29	Gives information to outsiders .44
Terminal action −.25	Courtesy to outsiders .44
Factor C: Complying with Suggestions Made by Others	Follows lead by outsiders .41
Concluding decision .73	Number of outsiders involved .31
Number of items attempted .68	Carelessness or minor error .30
Follows lead by subordinates .65	Awareness of poor work −.31
Terminal action .59	**Factor H: Directing the Work of Others**
Follows lead by superiors .50	Leading action .64
Follows pre-established procedure .48	Communicates by writing .59
Communicates by writing .45	Courtesy to subordinates .57
Number of words written .33	Gives directions or suggestions .47
Number of subordinates involved .31	Courtesy to outsiders .40
Gives directions or suggestions .31	Carelessness or minor error .31
Gives information to subordinates .28	Number of subordinates involved .28
Number of usual courses of action .27	Communicates by telephone −.30
Informality to subordinates .27	Tentative or definite plans only −.67

ability measures, and so on—was also available. The relation of the factor scores to these other variables is a matter of considerable interest. Therefore the intercorrelations of 120 variables were computed. The variables included in-basket category scores, ability measures, personality inventory scores, ratings, interest measures, tests of professional knowledge, and biographical items.

It is, of course, possible merely to compute the correlations between factor scores and other variables; but such an approach is possibly misleading because of the fact that the factors are substan-

Table 3

Second-Order Factors

Factor X: Amount of Work Done in Handling Items

Number of words written	.67
Number of usual courses of action	.65
Number of outsiders involved	.60
Gives directions or suggestions	.57
Number of subordinates involved	.57
Communicates by writing	.56
Leading action	.53
Gives information to subordinates	.52
Follows lead by superiors	.51

Factor Y: Preparation for Decision vs. Taking Final Action

Arrives at a procedure for deciding	.69
Requires further information for deciding	.64
Work scheduled for same or next day	.61
Discusses with subordinates	.60
Asks subordinates for information or advice	.56
Communicates face-to-face	.55
Initiates a new structure	.54
Work scheduled for same or next week	.54
Concluding decisions	−.52
Terminal action	−.62

tially correlated and hence contain variance which is shared by other factors. A factor-analytic approach to the problem was adopted, at the suggestion of Dr. Ledyard Tucker, which makes it possible, in effect, to determine the relationship of each variable to the part of each factor which is not shared by other factors. For example, *Amount of Work* influences in varying degrees the scores on all the eight factors; it would be desirable to learn the relationship between variables and factors with the effect of *Amount of Work* ruled out. The method employed resulted in the computation of coefficients which are proportional to the correlations with the unique part of each of the eight factors.

The procedure is as follows: the 120 x 120 matrix was factored. An orthogonal factor matrix composed of the first ten factors was

Table 4

Stages in Decision-Making

Stage in Decision-Making	In-Basket Score	Loading on Factor Y
1. Recognizes a problem		
2. Prepares to clarify the problem	Arrives at a procedure for deciding	.69
	Requires further information for deciding	.63
3. Initiates work on the problem	Work scheduled for same or next day	.61
	Discusses with subordinates	.60
	Asks subordinates for information	.56
	Leading action	.41
4. Organizes and judges facts and opinions	Conceptual analysis	.24
	Tentative or definite plans only	.16
	Delays, postpones	.15
5. Selects alternative solutions	Follows lead by superiors	.09
	Follows lead by subordinates	−.10
6. Decides and acts	Concluding decision	−.51
	Terminal action	−.62

rotated to form an oblique matrix having a factor structure as nearly as possible like that found for the original in-basket factor analysis. Coefficients were computed which reflect the relative relationship of each of the 120 variables to each of eight oblique reference vectors, each vector corresponding to one of the eight in-basket factors. These coefficients are proportional to the correlations with the unique portion of the corresponding factor. Similar estimates of correlations with second-order factors were computed. We shall merely indicate briefly a few salient findings.

Table 5 shows the relationships of several cognitive measures with in-basket factors. We see that both of the second-order factors (Columns 9 and 10) have fairly high relationships with the tests. *Amount of Work* is related to a variety of cognitive abilities, while *Preparation for Decision* relates especially to the School Administration test. The signs of the correlations in Column 10 show that high-ability

Table 5

Relationships of Cognitive Ability Tests to in-Basket Test Factors

	1 Exchanging Info.	2 Discussing	3 Complying w/ Sugg.	4 Analyzing Situation	5 Maintaining Rela.	6 Organizing Work	7 Resp. to Outsiders	8 Directing	9 Amount of Work	10 Prep. for Decision
Reasoning	.02	.03	.48	.34	-.15	.07	-.31	-.22	.28	.13
Subtraction and Multiplication	.43	-.14	.00	-.25	.14	.09	.12	-.26	.38	.21
Vocabulary	.39	-.14	.06	.15	.03	-.06	-.12	-.31	.33	.24
Concealed Figures	.04	.16	.47	.22	-.22	.11	-.13	-.24	.30	.24
Mathematics Aptitude	.06	.04	.49	.24	-.13	.18	-.17	-.30	.34	.16
School Administration and Supervision	.36	-.09	.15	.18	.01	.04	-.23	-.28	.41	.45
NTE Science and Mathematics	.07	.09	.48	.33	-.21	.02	-.27	-.27	.28	.19

people tend to prepare for decision rather than to take action.

The other columns show relationships with the unique parts of the eight in-basket factors—the part remaining after the variance due to second-order factors is removed. The coefficients in the first eight columns therefore cannot be attributed to *Amount of Work* or to *Preparation for Decision.*

There are a number of high positive coefficients, particularly in Columns 1 and 3. People who characteristically exchange information (Column 1) are high on Verbal and Number factors and on the test of school administration. The relationships with *Complying with Suggestions* (Column 3) involve a completely different set of tests, particularly tests of reasoning. Perhaps the compliance factor is not weak submission, but involves logical evaluation of suggestions.

Coefficients in Columns 7 and 8 are mostly negative. Those principals who were responsive to outside pressures and who were characterized by actively directing the work of their subordinates tended to be the less able principals.

Table 6 gives relationships between in-basket factors and some selected scores from Cattell's 16 Personality Factor Inventory. The personality scores do not predict the second-order factors; but there are a number of high relationships with the unique parts of the primary factors. Look at Column 5, for example. Principals who typically try to maintain good organizational relationships tend to be friendly, adventurous rather than shy, and free from anxiety and nervous tension. Look at Column 6. Principals who typically plan their work for specific days and hours tend to lack frustration tolerance and to be shy, suspicious, anxious, and nervous. Anxious people appear to exhibit a compulsive pattern of behavior in handling in-basket problems.

Table 7 shows relationships of in-basket factors with some biographical information items. Again the second-order factors are unrelated to the predictors, but the unique parts of the primary factors have high relationships with certain of the items. Years of college training has nothing to do with any of the factors; but age, experience, and sex do. *Complying with Suggestions* (Column 3) is typical of inexperienced young men. *Responding to Outsiders* (Column 7) is characteristic of experienced older women.

The simulation of a standard job in educational administration through the use of in-baskets has proved to be successful as a method of collecting records of administrative performance which can be

Table 6

Relationships of Personality Measures to in-Basket Factors

	1 Exchanging Info.	2 Discussing	3 Complying w/ Sugg.	4 Analyzing Situation	5 Maintaining Rela.	6 Organizing Work	7 Resp. to Outsiders	8 Directing	9 Amount of Work	10 Prep. for Decision
Friendly vs. Aloof	.21	−.09	−.29	−.28	.51	−.14	−.15	−.18	−.01	.01
Emotional Maturity vs. Lack of Frustration Tolerance	.15	.28	−.09	−.10	.12	−.36	.08	−.03	.12	.07
Dominance vs. Submission	−.14	.03	.12	.30	.14	.03	−.37	−.12	−.03	.09
Adventurous vs. Shy	.03	.19	−.26	.01	.50	−.33	−.23	−.07	−.02	.08
Emotional Sensitivity vs. Tough, Practical	.34	−.07	−.21	−.28	.22	−.11	.12	−.19	.10	.05
Suspicious vs. Trusting	−.30	−.16	.36	.18	.14	.45	−.13	.00	−.02	−.13
Sophistication vs. Rough Simplicity	−.12	−.10	.09	.30	.02	−.02	−.35	.01	−.08	−.03
Anxious Insecurity vs. Placid Self-Confidence	−.21	−.28	.25	.14	−.35	.55	−.01	.03	−.11	.00
Nervous Tension	−.21	−.30	.39	.22	−.30	.60	−.22	−.14	−.10	.04

Table 7

Relationships of Biographical Information to in-Basket Test Factors

	1 Exchanging Info.	2 Discussing	3 Complying w/Sugg.	4 Analyzing Situation	5 Maintaining Rela.	6 Organizing Work	7 Resp. to Outsiders	8 Directing	9 Amount of Work	10 Prep. for Decision
Experience in Education	.09	-.18	-.49	.01	.08	.04	.44	.28	.04	.01
Years of Academic Preparation	-.01	.02	.08	.08	-.08	-.01	-.15	.04	.03	.14
Age	.02	-.15	-.43	.05	.06	.02	.40	.28	.00	-.05
Sex (Male = 1, Female = 2)	.45	.17	-.60	-.42	.22	-.07	.50	-.03	.08	.13

scored reliably, and which yields scores which are useful in providing a better understanding of some of the dimensions of performance in such a situation. The method of factoring which was employed appears to be a powerful technique for isolating important aspects of behavior and examining their relationships with other measures.

11. system simulation —a fundamental tool for industrial engineering

DONALD G. MALCOLM

Vice President, Western Division, Operations Research Incorporated, Santa Monica, California

During recent years a new technique has come into prominence as an aid both in the task of training and in problem solving. This technique, called *System Simulation,* has been developed in both the military and industry by operations research and Industrial Engineering groups charged with making recommendations concerning complex planning problems and with developing training methods. A growing need for this thorough and scientific study, plus the availability of high speed electronic computers, has brought the concept of system simulation to the fore as a useful Industrial Engineering and management tool.

System simulation has the most useful property of permitting experimentation with and testing of certain policy, procedure and organization changes in much the same way as the aeronautical engineer tests his design ideas in the laboratory or the "wind tunnel." Simulation, long used as an engineering method is now being used to:

1. Study complex operating plans and management controlling systems for the purpose of designing better plans and/or systems.
2. Study and train people in the operation of complex tasks.

Reprinted in part from D. G. Malcolm, "System Simulation—A Fundamental Tool for Industrial Engineering," *Journal of Industrial Engineering,* 9 (1958), 177-187, with the permission of the author and the American Institute of Industrial Engineers.

3. Gain acceptance of proposed changes through better understanding of how a given system works or operates.

Simulation has application from very small day-to-day problems to complex management and industrial engineering problems requiring operations research teams and computers. As we shall see, simulation has the advantage of being easily understood, relatively free of mathematics and of often being quite superior to mathematical methods which may be too complex to apply or even not available. Another distinct advantage lies in the fact that simulation generally eliminates the need for costly trial and error methods of trying out a new operating concept on real flesh-and-blood and machines.

The purpose of this paper is to develop in a non-technical manner answers to the questions, What? How? Who? and Why?, facing the Industrial Engineer interested in what simulation may offer. Discussion is therefore directed to the following objectives:

1. To indicate the nature and utility of the method by means of an illustrative example.
2. To describe some industrial applications of simulation and to provide a partial bibliography.
3. To relate the method to more analytical approaches and discuss its role in "Installation Theory."[1]

One of the difficulties involved in the solution of problems of the broad nature referred to, is the compartmentalized thinking that organization structure and accounting methods tend to impose upon the managers of the affected departments. Each manager is motivated primarily by goals related to his own function which generally conflict with cost goals in other departments. The management of inventory is a well-known example of this class of problems.

In solving such problems top management generally arrives at a solution by compromise—a little bit for everyone and really not getting the best economic solution from the over-all company point-of-view. Since this is a well-known problem, let us briefly discuss the question it raises. How can we get at such problems where interactions between various elements of the problem or between various functions in the organization play such an important role in finding this best over-all solution, and, perhaps even more important, getting the solution accepted and implemented?

---

[1] Installation Theory has been defined as "study of the over-all most efficient way of introducing a change."

METHODS FOR ATTACKING SUCH PROBLEMS

There are three general courses of action open to us which are of value in different ways. Let us list these and then discuss each method briefly.

1. Experiment with the real facilities, machines and men.
2. Use formal mathematical analysis—construct equations describing the various alternatives.
3. Conduct simulated experiments, called *system simulation* here.

experiment with the real facilities, machines and men

Generally speaking, any idea that has been thoroughly studied is still not proven until it is tried out in the real situation. In using this method, suggested ideas or plans are brought forward for consideration as a result of cost studies of varying degrees of detail and refinement. Or, we may decide to emulate the practices of successful competitors and plan to do better through knowledge of their successes and mistakes.

In either event the basic task of study and analysis of the interactions involved by means of "models" is not performed. The suggested plan, when approved, is simply put into effect. If the plan proves to be inadequate a modification is made. Thus, as often happens, we end up "experimenting" with our own men, machines and facilities. While in many cases this is the only method available—*and it does get action*—there is the attendant confusion and cost of operating inefficiently for a long period of time while "testing" alternatives that may be avoided by the analysis or simulation approaches.

formal mathematical analysis

This is the most desirable and powerful approach. However, this method, which may be said to consist of writing equations that describe completely the problem area or system under study, is often too complicated to utilize effectively. Also, in many situations the mathematics have not or cannot be developed which will permit all the desired factors to be considered simultaneously. This is particularly true in the case of competitive problems.

Moreover, the mathematical method generally poses a distinct problem in communication. It is often hard to convince people that what a complex formula seems to say is really the best thing to do. There are many "if's" and "but's" that are hard to overcome in the process of getting change accepted. Thus "experimentation," as discussed above, generally still has to be performed. In cases where the first two methods have not given satisfactory results the method of *system simulation* is often useful.

simulated experiments—system simulation

In using this method the problem or system under study is first described as the sequence of individual operations to be performed. This may be called the "Flow Model" of the system. It is then necessary to have data indicating how the individual operations are interrelated and to have the frequency distribution of elapsed times for each individual operation for the different conditions to be explored.

Then inputs of such items as manpower, scheduling methods, or amounts of equipment, facilities, etc., are systematically varied. By consulting the time data mentioned above in a random manner, the over-all time for the sequence of operations can be determined. This process performed over and over simulates operation of the system and permits accruing such total system data as average equipment and manpower utilization, or inventory out-ages, delays, etc. Such outputs are then used to evaluate the desirability of the given input under test and in effect a simulated experiment has thus been conducted.

AN ILLUSTRATIVE EXAMPLE

Since the foregoing description is somewhat brief, a relatively simple yet practical example will be traced through to illustrate the concept and provide a vehicle for further discussion of the method and some applications that have been made in industry. This particular example has also been chosen to bring out the relationship of the simulation method to the mathematical method for treating the same problem.

the problem stated

Let us look at the following problem. We have a shop in which 20 machines run continuously for 24 hours per day 5 days per week. These machines experience breakdowns from time to time despite preventive maintenance practices. We have four repairmen on duty at all times and the machines are such that only one repairman can work effectively at a machine at a given time. Furthermore, the repairmen cannot be used for other than the repair task at hand. As managers, we are concerned over two observable facts which have come to our attention.

1. From time to time we note that there are more than four machines down simultaneously and we wonder if a fifth repairman would be a profitable investment in labor to avoid machine-waiting time.
2. We also note that there are many times when all repairmen are idle and that there are even more times when three and two repairmen respectively are idle. Therefore, we *also* wonder conversely, do we have *too* many repairmen and would not three repairmen be more satisfactory? Thus we have conflicting possibilities to study.

a rough analysis—solution by averages

Now suppose we have made studies which show that the average running time between breakdowns is ten hours and that on the average the necessary repairs require one hour to complete, i.e., the machine is down one hour out of every eleven total hours on the average.

This rough data indicates that from twenty machines we could expect 1/11 times 20 hours of work to arrive each hour. This turns out to be 1.82 hours of work each hour and we have available 4 man-hours to take care of this work. This would seem to indicate (if we are content with this analysis) that 4 men could take care of the repairs quite adequately and with no machines ever caused to wait on a repairman. Further, we might expect to find on the average that repairmen are idle approximately 54 per cent of the time

$$\left(\frac{4 - 1.82}{4} = .54 \right).$$

However, recent work sampling studies made in observation of the actual workmen indicate that the percentage of idle man time actually varies from 32 to 63 per cent and that machines wait for a repairman from 3.3 per cent to 1.1 per cent of the total available time. It is hard to pick out the best figures from the above utilization studies to use in our cost study. And how do we know what the effect of putting on or taking off an additional man would be?

Clearly, our rough analysis is not sufficient to evaluate the economics of utilizing another repairman. We could try to get an answer by experimenting with the real men and machines. To do this we would actually put on an additional man and after a period of time carefully measure how much better machine utilization we had achieved. Then if we weighted this against the cost incurred we could get a measure of improvement. Then, after awhile, we could cut back to three men and again measure the effects. While in effect this is the method we have been using, it is costly both in time and in money lost if we are not operating at the right solution now. As indicated, *system simulation* is a way of performing this "experimenting" in the laboratory without the costly and disturbing job of experimenting with the real people and equipment (which are continually changing anyway).

performing the simulation with three repairmen

To perform this simulated experiment we need data which we already have from records concerning the running time between repairs and the elapsed time in making the necessary repairs. Our operations analyst tells us that we have a chance of one in ten (probability of .1 in mathematical language) of machine breaking down in any given hour of operations.[2] An extensive study of the resulting repairs discloses the following:

40% of the repairs require $\frac{1}{2}$ hour to complete.
30% of the repairs require 1 hour to complete.
20% of the repairs require $1\frac{1}{2}$ hours to complete.
10% of the repairs require 2 hours to complete.

These data tell us that we have a 40 per cent chance of a given breakdown's requiring $\frac{1}{2}$ hour to repair, a 30 per cent chance of its requiring an hour to repair, and so on. With these data we are now ready to simulate what would happen if we were to use various numbers of repairmen. Let us start with *three*.

Our first task is to estimate how many machines will break down in a given hour of operation of our simulated system. To do this we could turn to a roulette wheel with ten numbers. It is quickly apparent why the term "Monte Carlo" method has become popular in describing an important aspect of *system simulation.*

Since our chances of having a breakdown were previously determined to be one chance in ten we can let any one of the ten digits represent a breakdown. We are assuming an unbiased wheel wherein

---

[2] A statistical analysis of the breakdowns is necessary to establish the appropriate probability statement.

the ball is as likely to land on one number as any other. In our example we shall arbitrarily assign the number *nine* to represent a breakdown.

Now rather than actually use this exciting device of chance, let us refer to a table of random numbers that has been painstakingly recorded by scientists for just such types of analysis. This table may be thought of as the record of many throws at the wheel. It is an unbiased listing that gives us numbers that are perfectly random. Fig. 1 represents a portion of such a table of random numbers.

TABLE OF RANDOM DIGITS   67

03300	87949 59115	26885 48261	76540 67250	69705 03936	27536 52568
03301	51343 98859	77231 10765	55295 34116	85842 97783	09346 90710
03302	21397 90842	30562 73877	98000 40627	50655 78125	48864 92845
03303	54696 95594	14946 57540	39628 54643	76085 86416	33326 89169
03304	53676 73107	27956 57494	20694 10757	86038 48807	58577 73570
03305	94874 80302	51391 61287	38416 15559	29084 00561	96030 74125
03306	78508 94303	87162 28094	47554 75403	48748 34074	88055 52322
03307	57623 65457	91297 51592	22052 84757	88940 58760	49212 66688
03308	01471 88847	22546 63509	90082 34417	27537 81276	78832 83479
03309	56630 31877	06048 64380	13625 26616	22899 65479	79981 20991

Figure 1   Table of random digits. (Reproduced with permission from "A Million Random Digits" by the Rand Corp., 1955, The Free Press, Glencoe, Ill.).

Since we have 20 machines, each with a chance for a breakdown, let us look at 20 numbers from this table as shown in the block at the left. In this group of 20 we observe that there are three number 9's. Thus three machines broke down during this hour.

The next question is, "How long do these repairs take?" To obtain this repair time we use the random number tables again. This time we assign digits 0-9 as follows:

1-4 incl. represent a ½ hour repair	(40%)
5-7 incl. represent a 1 hour repair	(30%)
8-9 incl. represent a 1½ hour repair	(20%)
0 represents a 2 hour repair	(10%)

Note that these are in the same proportion as our data concerning repairs as shown by the figures in parentheses.

Let us look at any three numbers to find out how long our three breakdowns require in repair. We shall use the last digit of each five digit number shown in the right inset. This gives us the 5, 8 and 4 shown underlined and our repairs will thus require 1, 1½ and ½ hours respectively. We have now *simulated* one hour of operation of our man-machine system and can keep score as shown in Fig. 2.

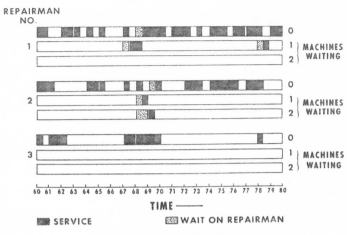

Figure 2 Time log of breakdowns.

The same method is continued until many such hours are simulated, building up the rest of the Fig. 2 as shown. As we go along we finally get into troublesome situations. In time period 68 for example, we found that more work arrived than we could conveniently handle with our work force. The waiting time due to this "unlucky" work load is shown as a shaded bar. This represents time during which the machine was down and could not be worked on because the repairmen were all occupied on other jobs that had arisen earlier.

Note that there is a lot of idle man time and *still* a fair amount of required idle machine time. Fig. 3 shows another portion of the simulation in which a greater amount of work happened to arrive. That is, more 9's came up in our "throw of the dice."

In Fig. 4, graphical portrayal of the arrival of this work is shown at the bottom, and the top of the graph indicates when the waiting time occurred. This figure depicts 100 hours of *system simulation*. At this point we have simulated the operations of this greatly simplified management system in the laboratory, without disrupting the organization by removing or adding an employee and without waiting until working habits settle down so that a real live time study would produce meaningful data.

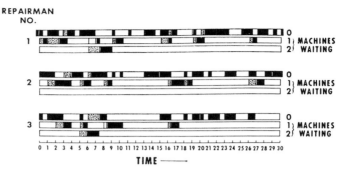

Figure 3   Time log of breakdowns.

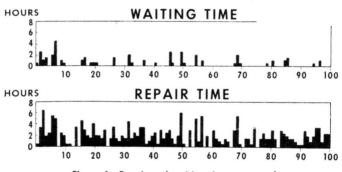

Figure 4   Repair and waiting time generated.

performing the simulation with 2, 4 and 5 repairmen—data resulting

We next perform simulation for 2, 4 and 5 repairmen in a similar manner. Table 1 indicates the data summarized from these simulations.

Examination of these data indicates the gain in machine utilization through employment of additional repairmen. We note that there is a smaller increase in machine running time as additional repairmen are used. At this point our simulation is completed and we are in a position to put costs on the data in such a way as to make a lowest cost solution.

Table 1

Data Reduction from Simulations	Number of Repairmen			
	2	3	4	5
Breakdowns per Hour, Ave.	1.78	1.95	1.97	1.97
Hours per Repair, Ave.	.994	.972	.970	.970
Machine Running Time— Percent	79.5	87.8	89.6	90.1
Idle Repairmen Time— Per cent	13.5	36.7	52.0	61.6

utilizing results of simulation in making a decision

While it is not our purpose to deal primarily with the economics involved in this illustrative example, perhaps one way in which the data can be used should be shown in the interest of making a complete example. Suppose in our example it is our intention to turn out a specific amount of production per week and that we will work on Saturdays, if necessary, in order to turn out this planned amount.

Suppose further that considering the overtime and standby labor involved, we have ascertained that idle machine time costs us $5.00 per hour. Our regular repairman rate is $2.50 per hour. Now with the data in Table 1 we can compute the cost per machine hour of operating with different numbers of repairmen.[3] Fig. 5 depicts the results of such computations.

In this case our decision is indicated quite clearly—we should change to three repairmen instead of the four currently used. From Fig. 5 we can also estimate the annual savings which turns out to be $4200 with the same total production possible. While this is a small amount, the relative size of the problem should be kept in mind. . . .

priority versus arrival scheduling of repairs

In the simulation as originally performed the repairs were performed in the exact order in which they arrived. The manager has suggested that the shorter repairs should always be performed first when several breakdowns occur at the same time. This is referred to as "priority" scheduling.

---

[3] C/machine hour $= \dfrac{r \cdot 2.50 + 5.00 \ (1 - \% \text{ machine running time})}{m}$ where:

r = number of repairmen, m = number of machines in group.

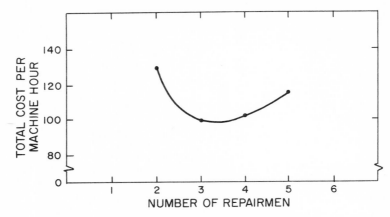

Figure 5   Total variable cost per machine hour.

To do this the simulation analyst must keep track of all the repairs arriving in any hour and assign them in accordance with the priority rule of "assign the shortest repairs" first. Several other rules might have been suggested, but let us consider the effect of this one by simulation. We perform the experiment in exactly the same manner except that we now apply the priority rule. When this has been completed for the various number of repairmen, we have data which are shown in Fig. 6.

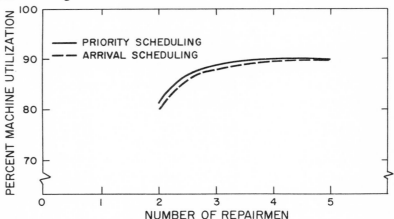

Figure 6   Machine utilization priority versus arrival scheduling.

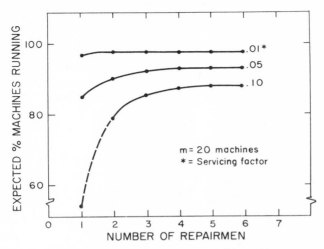

Figure 7   The effect of using more reliable machines.

We note that there is a slight gain in applying this priority rule. To evaluate the gain, we merely estimate the savings obtained versus the cost of having someone apply the scheduling required to obtain the savings. (It may not cost anything.) The manager is now in a position to evaluate how sophisticated a system he should employ in controlling his repair personnel.

the effect of introducing more reliable machines

Without belaboring this example, we again perform the simulation in the same manner except that we alter the probability of break-down in a given hour from .1 to .05 and to .01. This requires the use of two digit numbers from our table of random numbers to represent a breakdown. For example, we might let the numbers 00 to 04 represent the .05 probability of a breakdown. Otherwise the simulation is performed in exactly the same manner and results in developing operating curves such as shown in Fig. 7.

With this data we are in a position to evaluate the economics of purchasing more reliable machines. This example can also be thought of as being directly analogous to the loading or set-up time required in a job lot production shop. Here, repair time becomes set-up time. Thus we also have a method for evaluating the economies of more automatic machines.

THE ROLE OF THE COMPUTER

Up to this point the use of a computer in connection with the concept of simulation has not been mentioned. Generally speaking, most problems of any size worth exploring in any great detail will be most efficiently and economically handled through utilization of an appropriate electronic computer. The volume of detail and the number of hours that must be simulated in order to arrive at meaningful results generally demands that such a program be developed. In fact, even a problem of the size of the example, when extended to include the other conditions that we found desirable to make it more real, can be explored more efficiently and quickly if performed on an electronic computer.

In preparing the problem for the computer, the analyst generally prepares a logical Flow Diagram. This diagram shows the sequential steps involved in the problem or "system" under study and is useful in programing the computer.

INDUSTRIAL APPLICATIONS

Perhaps the most dramatic aspects of system simulation lie in its ability to reproduce the workings of large scale systems. While such ambitious programs are of more interest, it should be borne in mind that their success is dependent on having performed many smaller simulations for experience, upon adequate data and upon consideration of the many mathematical and statistical problems that are involved in construction of a feasible and economical model. Those considering broad full-scale models as panaceas in the decision-making area are well advised to engage in smaller projects at the outset. This will prevent certain disillusionment and make for a more meaningful research program.

12. computer simulation of peak hour operations in a bus terminal

NORMAN H. JENNINGS and JUSTIN H. DICKINS
The Port of New York Authority

The Port of New York Authority Bus Terminal presently serves 25,000,000 interstate bus travelers a year, most of whom are commuters between New York City and the suburban residential areas of New Jersey. As is the case with most urban rapid transit facilities, the controlling factor in design and operation is the peak-hour activity. This terminal was designed to accommodate up to 576 bus departures—about 26,000 outbound commuters—in the one peak hour of 5 to 6 P.M. on each week day. The terminal occupies an entire city block—200 feet x 800 feet—in mid-Manhattan where high real estate costs impose space economy. Its large-scale bus operations are compactly superimposed in a four-level building with direct ramp access to the Lincoln Tunnel which connects New York City with New Jersey. A three-acre automobile parking lot on the terminal's roof has capacity for over 450 cars.

Reprinted in part from Norman H. Jennings and Justin H. Dickins, *Management Science*, 5 (1958), 106-120, with the permission of the authors and The Institute of Management Sciences.

The authors wish to express appreciation to the staff at the Columbia University Watson Scientific Computing Laboratory for making available their I.B.M. 650 computer and auxiliary punched card equipment during the development phase of this project. In late 1957 the Port Authority installed its own I.B.M. 650 computer and the final production runs were made on this unit.

The authors wish also to thank the following individuals for their invaluable contributions to the project:

Mr. John Richard, Assistant Management Engineer, who assisted in the project's computations and analysis and organization of manuscript material; Mr.

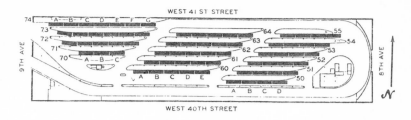

THE
PORT OF NEW YORK AUTHORITY
PORT AUTHORITY BUS TERMINAL
SUBURBAN BUS LEVEL

Figure 1

The top floor of the terminal is a suburban level for commuter bus traffic and the lowest floor is designed for long-route bus traffic. Two intermediate levels include ticket offices, baggage and waiting rooms, and concourses that allow interchange between the various levels. They also accommodate shops, stores, and other services for the convenience of the bus travelers.

The arrangement of the suburban level bus loading platform area is shown in Figure 1. Suburban buses enter the terminal at the west end and discharge their passengers on the long continuous unloading platform on the south side. When empty, the buses proceed around the east end of the terminal, then along the north roadway as necessary to enter their designated loading berths in the single-lane roadways between platforms.

A total of 72 starting berths is provided and it can be seen that all berths are in tandem along the individual platforms which vary in size from two berths to seven berths. The most common size of bus-loading platform contains five tandem berths. Due to the single-lane roadways it is readily apparent that any bus occupying a loading berth blocks entry to any berth ahead of it on the same loading platform. Bus-operating and employee-contract constraints prohibit the interchange of buses or drivers between routes, which means that each bus must load in its designated berth only.

Due to varying traffic conditions on bus routes to the terminal, suburban bus arrival times deviate randomly from their scheduled

Alan Steinberg, formerly Assistant Management Engineer, Port of New York Authority, who capably executed the major portion of all IBM programing and computer work in this study.

arrival times. Consequently, when a bus arrives in the loading area, its designated platform berth may be either vacant or occupied. Frequently, when its berth is vacant on arrival, the bus is denied immediate entry because it is blocked, or if ahead of schedule, it is withheld to avoid creating a block.

In each of these cases, the arriving buses require holding-space areas on the suburban level while awaiting platform berth access. During the commuter rush hour, peak volumes of bus arrivals generate bus waiting lines that cause critical bus traffic congestion in the holding-space areas.

As can be seen in Figure 1, these holding-space areas on the commuter level are extremely limited. The north wall has 7 such holding spots, the east wall 4, and the south wall 2—for a total of 13. Those on the north wall are further restricted in that the westerly 4 spots can only serve the westerly group of loading platforms. The major portion of the south wall cannot be used for this purpose since it is continuously needed for unloading operations.

Bus arrival deviations also affect another set of waiting lines in suburban level rush hour operation. Commuters arrive on the loading platforms in random patterns and accumulate in queues at the loading berths. Late buses lengthen the queues, aggravating commuters' delays.

Due to the direct relationship of bus blocking in the single-lane roadways and the lengths of bus and commuter waiting lines, the number of tandem berths per platform is a critical design factor.

Comprehensive scientific examination is required of the optimum relationship of the lengths of the waiting lines generated to the number of tandem berths on a single-lane loading platform. The result of such an examination will be of major assistance to management in determining the most efficient design to be incorporated in any future bus terminal construction.

It is impractical for economic and technical reasons to make a definitive study of the problem by empirical observations at the terminal. Adequate analysis of day-to-day probabilistic variations in waiting lines would require many weeks of costly sampling. On each platform bus arrival and departure schedules are fixed by bus operating policy. They are found to differ among loading berths on the same platform as well as between any two platforms. Neither the individual bus schedules nor the random arrival variations are subject to control for observation purposes. Hence, observed data would fail to provide a uniform basis for direct comparison of waiting lines on different platforms.

Our purpose here is to demonstrate the adaptability of a theoretical method using simulation techniques on a high-speed computer in the solution of this design problem.

A limited number of days of peak-hour suburban bus operation were observed at the terminal to obtain frequency distributions of commuter passenger and bus arrivals. With these as inputs to a logic which controls bus access to berths, the simulation method using Monte Carlo techniques was contrived. For any given bus departure schedule, the method generates a minute-by-minute sequence of commuter bus and passenger waiting line lengths throughout the peak hour.

By appropriate programing on the IBM 650 computer, many weeks of simulated operation on single or multi-berth platforms are calculated in a few hours. This computing speed and the method's flexibility permit ready investigation of several other aspects of bus terminal design and operation. Some of these are discussed later.

TECHNICAL PROCEDURES

The method employed to study the minute-by-minute picture associated with a given platform at the terminal consisted of two basic techniques. First, the Monte Carlo generation of typical arrival patterns of buses and of passengers; second, a series of logical tests and moves which "play" these generated inputs in a manner which simulates actual operations.

In order to define all of these activities completely, four mathematical models were found to be sufficient:

    I. A model to generate, in a realistic fashion, the number of passengers arriving in each minute.

    II. A model describing the arrival times of buses (relative to their scheduled departure time).

    III. A set of rules which governs the loading of buses.

    IV. A set of rules controlling entry and exit of buses from their assigned berth positions.

From these four models, and utilizing a preselected initial status, a "status report" is generated for the end of the first minute of operations. The interplay of the four models and their operation upon the "status" at the end of the first minute then produces the "status" at the end of the second minute, etc.; repeated applications thus completing the simulation.

For example, if a queue of x passengers were on the platform at the end of minute $t - 1$, and if y additional passengers arrived in accordance with Model I and, further if z passengers boarded in accordance with Model III, then there would be a queue of length $x + y - z$ at the end of minute t. The key to the entire operation, of course, is the construction of realistic and workable models.

THE FOUR MODELS

model I—passenger arrivals[1]

To find the number of passengers arriving in any given minute t_i:

1) Find $A(t_i)$, where $A(t)$ is the mean profile curve of passenger arrivals. (See Figure 2.)
2) Draw a single random observation from a Poisson having mean $A(t_i)$. This is the number of passengers arriving in minute t_i.

model II—bus arrivals

To find the arrival time of a bus which is scheduled to depart from the terminal at a given time t.

1) Draw a random observation from a normal (Gaussian) distribution having mean $= -9$ and standard deviation $= 5$.
2) Add the scheduled departure time to the above selected random draw. This gives the arrival time of the bus.

A sample set of observed data and the corresponding fitted normal curve are shown in Figure 3.

model III—loading of buses[2]

1) If no bus is available, or it a bus is available but already has 46 passengers loaded, do not load any passengers.

---

[1] Standard data taking procedures used at the terminal provide passenger arrival statistics in the "profile" form shown in Figure 3. Some of the tests used to verify the model were a) Chi-square test of individual minutes to assure validity of Poisson assumption. b) Tests of actual daily total arrivals to see if they could be generated by the model. c) Tests of residuals after deducting $A(t)$ for serial correlation. Although the occurrence of the Poisson was extremely convenient for testing purposes, the tabular method used for random draws precludes any real need for an analytic function in the actual running of the computer program.

[2] Actual loading schemes differ in their loading rates according to whether

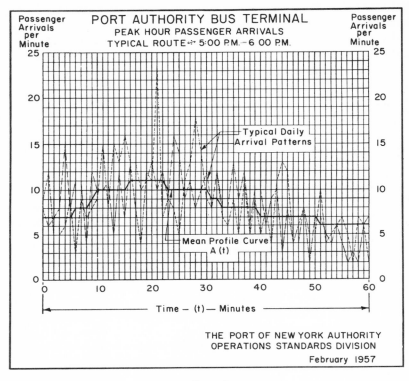

Figure 2

2) If a bus is available for loading and it has fewer than 46 passengers already loaded, then load the lesser of:
   a) 14 passengers
   b) The number of passengers on the platform (including current minute arrivals).

model IV—bus dispatching

The model employed for simulating dispatching on a two-berth single-lane platform with uniform headway is best described directly

passengers pay fares on entering or leaving buses. The pay enter scheme used in this model was found to be quite common at the terminal.

Many passengers are observed to be reluctant to board a bus in which all seats are taken. The loading rates of passengers willing to stand were found to be erratic. These rates are adequately simulated in the model by setting a bus loading cut-off value about equal to a typical commuter bus seating capacity.

in the mathematical terms used for programing. First the necessary variables or indicators are defined: In our approach seven (7) indicators were established which, in proper combinations, are capable of describing the status of all buses at any minute. These were as follows:

$t =$ current time ($t = 0$ is taken at 5:00 P.M.)
P_A describes the condition of the A berth as follows:
  $P_A < 0$ indicates empty berth.
  $P_A \geqq 0$ indicates a bus is present in berth A, and has been in berth for P_A minutes,
$D_A =$ the number of A buses that have already departed.
$H_A =$ the number of A buses in the holding area.

Definitions for P_B, D_B and H_B which pertain to B buses, follow logically.

The term "dispatching," as used here, is meant to include the decisions involved in governing entry into the berths as well as exit therefrom. Bus dispatching procedures vary according to such factors as the headway (i.e., interval between consecutive scheduled bus departure times), number of berths, number of buses in the team (i.e., all buses with the same scheduled departure time) and practices of bus dispatching personnel. The dispatching logic described reflects a very common situation and illustrates the general mathematical description of typical bus dispatching policy.

Our initial conditions assume empty berths at $t = -5$ ($P_A = P_B$ $= -99$ for convenience) and first schedule departure time at 5:00 ($t = 0$). Subsequent departures are scheduled at, say, W minute intervals (5:00 $+ W$; 5:00 $+ 2W$; . . .) and both A and B routes have identical departure schedules. This permits consideration of an A bus and a B bus collectively as a "team" if they have the same scheduled departure time.

Let us consider some of the moves of the game:
To advance "time-slice" by one minute:

$t \rightarrow t + 1$ (Time changed to next minute)

$P \rightarrow P + 1$ (Elapsed time of bus on platform increased by one minute)

To indicate the entry of a bus into the terminal:

$H \rightarrow H + 1$ (Number of buses in holding area increased by 1)

To indicate movement of a bus from the holding area into a berth:

$H \rightarrow H - 1$ (Number of buses in holding area decreased by 1)
$P \rightarrow 0$ (This indicates that a bus has just moved in)

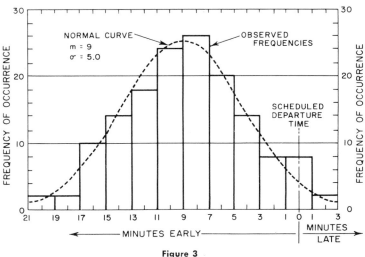

PORT AUTHORITY BUS TERMINAL

TYPICAL DISTRIBUTION OF
BUS ARRIVAL TIMES

Figure 3

To indicate departure of a bus:

$P \rightarrow -99$ (All negative values indicate empty berth)
$D \rightarrow D + 1$ (Number of departures increased by 1)

DISPATCHING DECISIONS

Not only do the seven indicators provide all the necessary imple-
ments for making the "moves" of the game, but they serve also as
the medium for making all necessary dispatching decisions. For example, the decision to move a *"B"* bus out involves three dichotomies:

1) Is there free access to exit from the platform; i.e., Is the *A*
berth vacant? This can be expressed mathematically as follows:

$$P_A < 0?$$

2) Has the *"B"* bus's scheduled departure time arrived, i.e.,

$$t \geqq WD_B?$$

where W is the headway? (A bus in the ith team, according to the ground rules stated, is scheduled to depart at $(i-1)W$. When a bus from the ith team is in berth, then $D = (i-1)$.

3) Is there a sufficiently loaded "B" bus in the berth? (A bus is considered loaded after three minutes on platform provided its scheduled departure time has arrived. This is empirically valid.) I.e.,

$$P_B \geqq 3?$$

This three-test sequence is adequate for simulating departure decisions[3] on a two-berth platform. Our general program is designed to simulate platforms with as many as nine berths. Although decisions

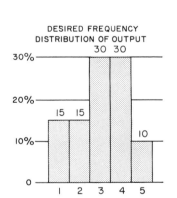

CONVERTING RANDOM DIGITS
INTO "RANDOM DRAWS"
TABLE-LOOK-UP METHOD

DESIRED FREQUENCY
DISTRIBUTION OF OUTPUT

TABLE USED TO ACHIEVE SPECIFIED FREQUENCY DISTRIBUTION OF OUTPUT

INPUT	OUTPUT
00-14	1
15-29	2
30-59	3
60-89	4
90-99	5

Figure 4

for more than two berths per platform become many times more complex than the one illustrated, the principal feature, sequential testing of dichotomies, remains the same.

---

[3] More difficult decisions are concerned with the question of admitting a bus into its berth. In addition to the problem of physical ability to enter the berth, the dispatching logic must include some mechanism for evaluating the risk of allowing a bus to enter if there is an imminent likelihood of thus creating a "block" in subsequent minutes. For example, in a two-berth problem, a "B" bus arriving ahead of its "A" mate will be temporarily held out. It would not be allowed to enter until its "A" mate arrived or until further delay would jeopardize its own ability to depart on schedule.

METHOD USED TO OBTAIN RANDOM DRAWS

A two-step procedure was utilized for obtaining the random draws required by Models I and II. First, random digits were generated internally using von Neumann's mid-square method and starting with 1111111111. (These digits have already been tested by the IBM Group at Los Alamos [2] and in addition, the programming required on a medium scale computer is trivial.) Second, two-digit random numbers were used to enter tables (constructed as indicated by Figure 4) to arrive at the random draws.[4]

RESULTS

As the computer simulates each minute of operation, it is programed to "read-out" a status report for the end of that minute. As illustrated in Figure 5, these minute-by-minute status reports portray the full history of events for the time period studied. The particular history shown in the figure was selected to demonstrate some of the intricacies of the dispatching logic which must be used even on a two-berth platform because of the single-lane restriction. A number of these situations are footnoted and are discussed beneath the diagram.

It may be noted that there are no data appearing in the tabulation which directly express the on-platform waiting time of the 924 passengers. The total of the "waiting line" column would give the total passenger-minutes of waiting time, and dividing by the number of passengers would, of course, give the average waiting time. However, to explore the "maximum" waiting time it is necessary, for all practi-

---

[4] There are many different methods for obtaining random draws from a specified population. These range in convenience from borrowing a prepunched deck of cards (1) to computation of the cumulative inverse distribution function or specialized methods such as suggested by von Neumann (3) and others. The tabular technique utilized in this study is particularly suitable for the operations researcher equipped with a medium or large scale computer. The method is economical since most medium and large scale computers have a "table-look-up" or "channel-search" operation code. This makes the conversion from random digits to random draws a one or two step program. In addition, and of great importance, is the fact that the method is suited to both nonanalytic and analytic distributions. The precision of the method is usually adequate for operations research problems. The tabular method becomes impractical if small class intervals, wide ranges, or certain types of changing parameters make storage of the tables a problem from a space standpoint.

M O D E L   O U T P U T

Time	Bus Arrival A	B	Hold Spots A	B	Passenger Arrivals A	B	Passengers Loaded In Bus A	B	Waiting Line A	B
4:55a		1	0	1	3	8			3	8
4:56			0	1	4	5			7	13
4:57b			0	0	3	1		14	10	
4:58c	1		1	0	4	2		16	14	
4:59		1	1	1	4	8		24	13	
→ 5:00d			0	1	9	1	14		13	1
5:01e	1		1	1	15	2	28		14	3
5:02			1	1	12	8	42		12	11
5:03			0	0	12	6	14	14	10	3
5:04			0	0	11	4	28	21	7	
5:05	1		1	0	6	12	41	33		
5:06			1	0	10	6	51	39		
→ 5:07f			0	0	7	9	7			9
5:08			0	0	5	13	12			22
5:09g		1	0	0	6	7	18	14		15
5:10			0	0	10	17	28	28		18
5:11			0	0	8	9	36	42		13
5:12			0	0	8	10	44	56		9
5:13			0	0	9	9	53	56		18
→ 5:14			0	0	7	11			7	29
5:15	1		0	0	8	12	14		1	41
5:16	1		1	0	8	9	23			50
5:17			1	0	7	4	30			54
5:18			1	0	8	13	38			67
5:19		1	1	0	5	5	43	14		58
5:20			1	0	5	5	48	28		49
→ 5:21h			1	0	9	6		42	9	41

Figure 5

---

a. Minutes 4:55, 4:56—"B" bus held out until 3 minutes before its scheduled

161

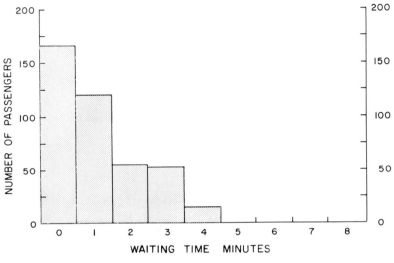

SUMMARY OF PASSENGER WAITING TIMES ON
THE "A" BERTH OF A 2 BERTH PLATFORM
TAKEN FROM ONE TYPICAL SAMPLE OF
PEAK HOUR OPERATION

Figure 6

cal purposes, to compute the waiting time for each individual passenger.

The computer program used in this study included instructions to generate a histogram of on-platform waiting times at the end of each simulation "run." By inspection of this histogram, maximum waiting

---

departure time to avoid blocking late arriving "A" bus schedule for same time of departure.

b. Minute 4:57—"B" bus sent into berth and loaded despite lack of "A" bus, 3 minutes before schedule departure time.

c. Minute 4:58—"A" bus blocked out by loading "B" bus.

d. Minute 5:00—"A" bus team mate of departed "B" bus sent in and loaded for 3 minutes. "B" bus of next team held out awaiting his "A" bus team mate.

e. Minute 5:01—Only 14 of 15 passengers arriving this minute for "A" bus can be loaded. See also "B" bus in minute 5:10.

f. Minute 5:07—"A" bus sent in immediately even though team mate "B" bus is late because "A" bus loading cannot block out "B" bus.

g. Minute 5:09—"B" bus sent directly into berth on arrival.

h. Minute 5:21—Late "B" bus held beyond scheduled departure time to load at least 3 minutes. Next "A" bus blocked out till following minute.

time for each run is determined. The on-platform passenger waiting time histogram for the "A" berth in the run illustrated in Figure 5 is shown in Figure 6.

The application of the foregoing methodology permitted the ready evaluation of the influence of platform length on passenger service and holding space requirements (see Figure 7). It is readily apparent

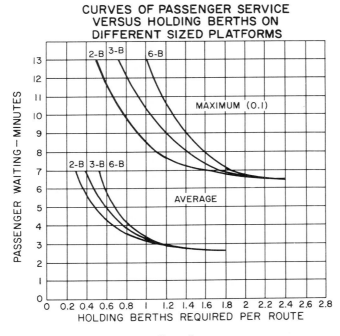

Figure 7

that, with equal holding space facilities, passenger service deteriorates as platform length increases. To state it differently—as platform lengths increase, more holding space per berth is required to maintain the same level of passenger service.

Figure 8 shows for different platform lengths the holding spaces required for 12 bus loading berths when maximum (0.1) passenger delay is limited to eight minutes. It is significant to note that 2 six-berth platforms require 50 per cent more holding space than 6 two-berth platforms to provide equivalent service to the same number of patrons within the same time period. These numerical values relate only to the specific assumptions of this simulation.

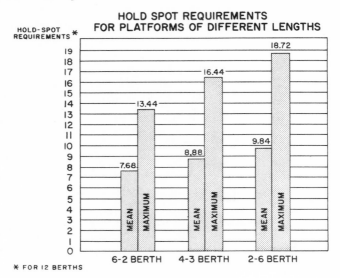

Figure 8

OTHER APPLICATIONS AND CONCLUSION

The original computer program used in this study was written with the single goal of determining the lengths of passenger waiting lines and bus queues for single lane platforms of different lengths, and assumes no changes in current bus operating practices. It is apparent, however, that this full simulation suggests other problems which might be approached. Some of these may have implications even more far-reaching than those of the problem as originally phrased.

For example, the **m** and σ associated with the bus arrival times are at least partially under the control of the bus operators. Changes to **m** can obviously be brought about by altering arrival schedules; changes to σ can, to some extent, be brought about by en-route dispatchers. This immediately suggests the very general problem: What combination of **m** and σ (within the attainable domain) will optimize operations?

More likely to produce results quickly, however, are the problems associated with the policies of a particular bus operator. Two such problems immediately suggest themselves. First, what sort of schedule (how many buses and at what times) is optimum for given passenger arrival patterns and berth configurations? Second, what is the optimum loading system (pay enter or pay leave) and dispatching policy? (Several current decisions, particularly, how long to hold up a whole team for a late bus, are worthy of further study).

In conclusion, it can be seen that what has been accomplished is somewhat more than simply evaluating the effect of the length of a single-lane bus platform. While this problem has been answered in a form suitable for design utilization in pending construction, the mechanism used for the solution, i.e., a flexible computer program for simulating the complete peak hour, is perhaps of even more significant value. The range of hypothetical floor plans and operating schemes which can be evaluated is limited only by the resourcefulness of those framing the proposals. With the Monte Carlo method, such proposals can be examined and tested, avoiding disruption of service that would result from protracted trial-and-error experimentation in actual operations.

references

1. Blanch, G. and E. C. Yowell, "A Guide to Tables on Punched Cards," *Mathematical Tables and Other Aides to Computation*—V, No. 36, Nat'l Bur. of Stds., Inst. for Numerical Analysis, L. A. Cal., October 1951.
2. Hammer, Preston C., "The Mid-Square Method of Generating Digits," *Monte Carlo Method*, U. S. Department of Commerce, p. 33, National Bureau of Standards; USGPO June 1951.
3. von Neumann, John, "Various Techniques Used in Connection with Random Digits" (Summary written by George E. Forsythe) *Ibid.* (2).

13. simulation as an aid in model building

R. P. RICH
Applied Physics Laboratory,
The Johns Hopkins University

When a complex situation is to be analyzed it is sometimes thought that the first step is the construction of a mathematical model. In practice, however, the construction of a mathematical model is far from the first step. By the time a really suitable model has been constructed, in many cases, most of the hard work has already been done. Once the model has been constructed it can usually be analyzed and verified by standard techniques recorded in the literature and taught in recognized academic fields. The steps leading up to the model, except for some concerned with the collection of data, do not share these advantages.

The present paper attempts to show one way in which the task of model building can be made easier. A specific example illustrates the use of a device which simulates the physical situation to be analyzed. The particular example chosen does not have wide applicability, but it does illustrate a number of points which may be of general interest.

Perhaps I should say a few words about why a paper dealing with a simulator was included in a discussion of war games. The situation dealt with in the example is a military one, but that is merely coincidental. The important point is that a war game set-up is itself a simulator; it is customarily used in situations where the element of

Reprinted from R. P. Rich, "Simulation as an Aid in Model Building," *Operations Research*, III (1955), 15-19, with the permission of the author and the Operations Research Society of America.

Presented at the Session on the Use and Value of War Game Methods in Solving Operations Research Problems at the Washington meeting of the SOCIETY on November 20, 1954.

emulation is thought to be particularly important, and the use of opposing teams tends to emphasize this element of the situation. But this element of emulation seems at least as easy to simulate as many of the other elements which must be taken into account. The fact that the simulator here described does not include human opposing teams, therefore, is not an important point of difference. From the present point of view, then, a war game is just a special type of simulator, with the opposing teams so many parts of the machine. It is subject to the same mode of criticism and adaptable to the same ends as any other simulator. Some of these ends can be illustrated by the following example.

A SIMPLE AIR-DEFENSE SIMULATOR

The problem was that of evaluating anti-aircraft guided missiles in the air defense of naval units. For our present purpose it is sufficient to consider a very simple tactical situation in which a single ship defends itself from air attack by using its own missile batteries.

The simulator consisted of a sheet of plywood four feet square. This was faced with a sheet of wallboard to take map tacks. A sheet of heavy paper was fastened over the wallboard so that pencil marks could be made as convenient. A horizontal projection of the course of the attack was formed on the surface so provided, as illustrated.

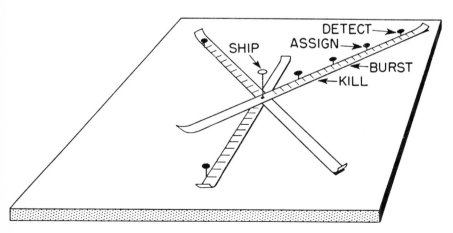

Figure 1   Air defense simulator.

Each attacking aircraft was represented by a strip of teletype tape marked with the aircraft speed, altitude, and type. Timing marks were put on the tape at five-second intervals. The distance between marks was the scale distance traveled by the plane in five seconds. The attack was set up by fastening ten of these target strips to the board, converging on the ship's position. The time over target for each aircraft was adjusted by sliding its strip along its axis until the desired time mark coincided with the ship's position. The position of each plane at any time during the attack could then be determined by locating the corresponding timing mark on its strip. The target paths and timing marks could of course have been drawn with pencil directly on the board but the strips were used repeatedly for various attacks, and their use reduced the time required to set up a new attack.

Target detection by the ship's search radar was simulated as follows. A graph was drawn showing the cumulative probability of detecting an incoming target as a function of range. From this the range at which the probability reached any given value could be read off. A strip of paper was prepared with a mark for each per cent of probability at the correct scale distance from the index mark. For each aircraft in turn a two-digit number was read from a table of random numbers, the same two-digit number was located on the radar detection strip, and a light blue map tack was put in the target strip at the corresponding distance from the ship. Of course no target was considered for assignment to a missile battery until after the time indicated by this map tack on the target strip.

A dark blue map tack was put in the target strip at the timing mark corresponding to the time when the target was assigned to a missile battery in accordance with the assumed firing doctrine.

A yellow pin was used to indicate the time when the salvo reached the target. The time interval between the two events included the battery acquisition time, the missile time of flight, and various minor time delays. The acquisition time was determined for each salvo by reading another random number from the tables and comparing it with the appropriate distribution function.

For each type of target used a graph was drawn showing the probability of kill as a function of the time after interception. A two-digit random number was compared with this graph to determine whether the target was killed, and if so, at what time the kill took place. The range corresponding to that time, as determined from the target strip, was then compared with the bomb release line for the aircraft speed and altitude being used to see whether or not the kill took place before bomb release.

After a little practice two people could run about 30 attacks of ten planes each in a working day. The scheme was simple in conception and workable in practice. No difficulty was encountered except the ever-present one of gathering the necessary data. The only thing that makes so simple a device worthy of mention at all is the somewhat surprising fact that it could prove as useful as it did.

PURPOSES SERVED BY THE SIMULATOR

The first purpose served by the simulator exercise was to provide a nucleus for collecting data. The need for each item and the most suitable form for it was clearly defined in the preparation for the runs. The nature of the expected attack, cumulative probability of detection for the search radar, distribution of tracking-radar acquisition times, delays in the missile system, missile kill probabilities as a function of range, target type and time after burst, bomb-release distances as a function of aircraft speed and altitude, all had to be determined, estimated or guessed. It would of course have been obvious even without the simulator that some of these items would be needed before numerical answers could be obtained. But some of the details could easily have been overlooked for some time if they had not been spotlighted in the process of writing down the rules of the game. The probability of death as a function of time after intercept, for instance, had received very little attention before the simulator emphasized its importance.

The second and perhaps the most important purpose served by the exercise was that of demonstrating patterns within what at first appeared to be chaos. After watching only a few runs it became apparent, for instance, that the engagement could be divided into a transient phase and a steady state. Investigation showed that each of these phases was governed by its own simple law, and that the two depended in quite different ways upon the tactical parameters. The number of transient engagements, for example, is roughly inversely proportional to target speed, while the number of steady-state engagements is independent of target speed and proportional to the time-spread of the attack. By such indications as this the simulator led naturally and directly to a mathematical formulation of the problem.

The third purpose served by the simulator arises from the function and position of the operations-research group in a larger complex. It is not enough to be able to find the answer and to be able to demonstrate it to one's own satisfaction. The same answer must also be made convincing to the people who are to make use of it, and this usually requires a different level of ideas and a different terminology. In the case under discussion, the simulator included in an obvious fashion operations already familiar to naval officers. The basic data and assumptions could be discussed in terms of their simulator analogs with few difficulties of translation. Furthermore, the relation between the simulator and the mathematical formulation was so direct that the simulator formed a strong and dependable bridge, firmly anchored at both ends, between the officers' past experience and the new theory.

The fourth purpose, and perhaps the least important from the present point of view, is the one which frequently comes first to mind when the subject of simulators is raised. That is the use of the simulator as a computing device to provide numerical answers. The device here described is too slow to be very useful in this role, but it was occasionally used as a check on computational approximations. The important point is that the simulator showed the way to a simple and reasonably accurate model which made it possible to get the desired answers by direct computation rather than by further simulation.

CONCLUSIONS

The example above emphasizes the fact that the terms "simulator" and "Monte-Carlo method" do not necessarily imply a large-scale digital computer and several weeks or months of programing time. The simulator here described was quickly assembled from available materials and had essentially completed its job within a few days from first inception. It is true that a simulator which is to serve as a computer should have a high-speed capability, and there is no intent here to minimize the importance of this function in situations where it is appropriate.

But there are other important functions that a simulator can perform for which the hardware requirements are much more modest. It can serve as a focus in the collection of data, as an aid in the construction of a mathematical model, and as a useful bridge between operations and research. The cost of such simulators in time, money, and manpower is so small, and their advantages in the early stages of study are so great, that they appear to deserve much fuller exploitation and discussion than they have enjoyed in the past.

14. the Systems Research Laboratory's air-defense experiments[1]

ROBERT L. CHAPMAN, JOHN L. KENNEDY,
ALLEN NEWELL and WILLIAM C. BIEL[1]

* * *

A system's environment can be inferred from, and its actions controlled by, information—a vital commodity to any organization. Man can discover meaningful patterns in information, invent response alternatives, and translate decisions into information for directing a system's actions. His capacity to modify his inferences and responses in order to satisfy a goal is unique. If an organization is to perform efficiently over a range of changing conditions, then the employment of its resources must be adjusted to particular circumstances. This would imply utilizing men who can make such adjustments.

Exploiting the ability of men in organizations to learn requires, of course, understanding organizational adaptation. It was in an attempt

Reprinted in part from Robert L. Chapman, John L. Kennedy, Allen Newell, and William C. Biel, "The Systems Research Laboratory's Air Defense Experiments," *Management Science,* 5 (1959), 250-269, with the permission of the authors and the Institute of Management Sciences.

This paper is a revision of a portion of a symposium presented at the American Psychological Association meetings in San Francisco in September, 1955 (RAND Papers 657, 658, 659, and 661). The authors wish to thank John O'Connell, Malcolm A. Palmatier and Leonard J. Savage for their helpful criticisms and Donna Bengtson, Lou Lansing and H. F. W. Perk for their work in the illustrations.

[1] The work reported was conducted while the authors were associated with the RAND Corporation. Robert L. Chapman is now with The Ramo-Wooldridge Division of Thompson-Ramo-Wooldridge Corporation; John L. Kennedy at Princeton University; Allen Newell with The RAND Corporation and The Carnegie Institute of Technology; and William C. Biel with The System Development Corporation.

to derive knowledge of that phenomenon that four of us—three psychologists and a mathematician—studied an air-defense direction center in the Systems Research Laboratory of the RAND Corporation from 1952 to 1954.

But to study the adaptation process in a real-life organization is very difficult. A direction center under actual attack, for example, is hardly the time or place for research. Even in peacetime operation, it is almost impossible to observe all activities of a real-world center. Controlling the air traffic and other aspects of the environment would be prohibitive.

So we tried to get as close an approximation to full-scale, real-life organizational behavior as we could in the laboratory. To do so, we had to *simulate* the environments. To get behavior worth studying, we tried to make the simulated environments genuine enough for the crew to respond to them as if they were real.

Because we wanted to explore how a crew might use the resources it had more effectively, we decided not to vary either the kind or amount of equipment (the physical environment) or such conditions as operation policies (the cultural environment). Instead, we manipulated task conditions (the task environment) to stimulate organizational adaptation as well as test its capabilities.

In order to facilitate learning, we fed back performance results in an immediate report that was pertinent, objective and accurate.

But it would not be sufficient merely to observe the over-all output of the center in a variety of tasks, however well simulated and planned. To understand how an organization adapts, we needed to see "inside," to get access to its detailed operations. In the direction center, changes in the use of information are exposed in what crew members say to each other, not confined exclusively to the impenetrable mental gyrations of a few key decision-makers.

As we looked back at the history of organizational research we noted that there had been much exploration of *ad hoc* hypotheses—much data had been accumulated but not integrated. We felt that the problem should be tackled differently: by looking at the whole to find significant variables rather than by examining variables separately and postponing their integration.

So the air-defense experiments were more a *search* for a framework for comprehending organizational behavior than tests of particular hypotheses.

casey, cowboy, cobra and cogwheel

Our first experiment, Casey, can best be described as a very profitable failure. We first underestimated the crew's capacity to learn by designing a series of task situations that turned out to be trivial rather than difficult. In trying to provide a challenging situation, we then broke the organization. (Interestingly enough there was no emotional upset; crew members continued to go through the same motions. But like a car with a worn-out clutch, operation had no functional effect. The crew had become disengaged from its task environment.)

These two mistakes, however, gave us the leverage to design a more appropriate sequence of task situations for the Cowboy experiment, which used military personnel in contrast to the college students of the first experiment.

By this time, the results had provoked a demand for application of the system training principles (as the off-the-top laboratory findings came to be called). This demand has been met by the establishment of the System Development Corporation, formerly a part of RAND, that consists of several very large digital computers surrounded by well over a thousand people—all of this devoted to improving air-defense effectiveness.

The third and fourth experiments, Cobra and Cogwheel, with other military crews, provided additional evidence about organizational development but were conducted mainly for orientation purposes.

In the course of trying to find the variables for predicting system performance, we had found that an essential factor—human learning —could be rather handily manipulated to make a lot of difference in the right direction. But system training is only one of the possible values of these explorations. There are, we believe, many other implications for the design and management of military systems and industrial organizations.

Instead of presenting just the bare facts, we should like to describe the air-defense experiments as a *search* for understanding of organizational behavior. Because, so far as we are concerned, a scientific investigation is not the cold-blooded, straight-forward, logical process that texts proclaim. It's an adventure. Sheer scientific excitement arises from the unexpected event, from the obvious assumption that's very wrong, from the hunch that pans out, from the sudden insight, and from the invention that covers the unanticipated procedural gap. The fact is that as organizations took form before our eyes, their struggle determined ours. We had to continue to circumscribe their machinations with experimental control, to devise techniques for observation, to try to comprehend their behavior. We were aided with the last of these by a curious circumstance. We found that to study an organization in the laboratory we, as experimenters, had to become one. (And we can truthfully add we'd rather see than be one.) As a consequence, to our objective observations were added intimate experiences in our own developing organization.

the air-defense direction center

The job of a direction center is to defend against enemy air attack. To do this, it maintains radar surveillance over its area of responsibility, identifies aircraft as friendly or hostile, and directs interceptor aircraft against hostile planes. Its successes and failures can be readily evaluated by the number of bombs dropped on targets in its area.

The center is an organization of about forty Air Force officers, noncoms, and airmen. Surveillance personnel watch radarscopes, phoning the positions of planes they see to a central display where these tracks are plotted. Meanwhile, friendly planes scheduled to be in the area have filed flight plans with the Civil Aeronautics Authority which forwards them to the direction center. The positions predicted by flight plans are compared with the radar tracks on the central display. Tracks that cannot be matched against "friendly" flight plans are called unknown.

Interceptors are ordered to take off and are directed toward unknown aircraft by the controllers. Once the aircraft type and serial number are visually determined by the interceptor pilot, the direction center may be able to verify that the unknown is, in fact, friendly. But, if the unknown's identity remains suspicious, or if he commits a hostile act, the officer in charge of the center—the senior director—may order the interceptor to open fire. At the same time, he may put the entire defense system and the country as a whole on an emergency alert.

The center receives partial information about the air traffic over its area from its radar sets (because of range and line-of-sight limitations, planes too far away or on the other side of an intervening mountain cannot be detected) and information about scheduled friendly traffic from the Civil Aeronautics Authority. Against the pattern of normal traffic, which is determined by the economic geography of the region and CAA rules, an enemy attack may appear. Thus, the

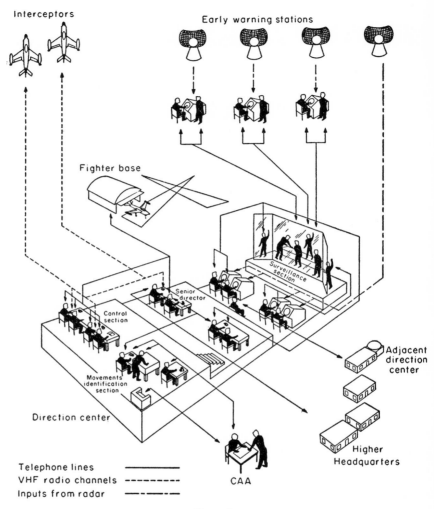

Interceptors

Early warning stations

Fighter base

Surveillance section

Senior director

Control section

Movements identification section

Direction center

Adjacent direction center

Higher Headquarters

CAA

Telephone lines ————————
VHF radio channels ------------
Inputs from radar —·—·—·—

Figure 1

This simplified model emphasizes aspects of the direction center's operation not readily seen in the previous schematic of functions: the physical arrangements within the center and the complex communication net (consisting of telephone lines, VHF radio channels, and radar inputs) that linked crew members to each other and to the external embedding organizations. Much of the communication within the center itself is either visual or by face-to-face conversations.

input to the center contains detailed, redundant information about a few very important events and many unimportant events in its task environment.

The crew's physical environment includes its tools for coping with task events: the information-gathering equipment (radar sets), the communications net (radios and telephones), information storage aids (central displays and written records), and its response equipment (interceptor aircraft and their weapons).

A miscellany of poorly-understood influences that tone the crew's behavior make up its cultural environment: individual abilities, habits, aspirations, traditions, language, likes, dislikes and beliefs about many other aspects of air-defense operations and Air Force life in general.

SIMULATING THE PHYSICAL ENVIRONMENTS

The main requirement for simulating the physical environment was that the tools given the crew be a close functional approximation to those of a real direction center. We tried as best we could to copy the physical layout, the communication net, the central displays, and general atmosphere of a particular center. Several major problems in simulating the physical environment deserve special mention.

the early-warning stations

The particular center we chose to study had subsidiary early-warning stations that extended its radar coverage over its area of responsibility. These early-warning stations report the aircraft they see to the center but have no other functions; identification and control of interceptors is carried out by the center.

At first we intended to study just the direction center itself. The early-warning stations were only to be simulated. Members of the staff, reading from prepared scripts, phoned early-warning information into the direction center.

It became painfully clear, after a few hours of operation in the training period of the first experiment, that the experimenters' role as early-warning stations was untenable. Crew members on the other end of the telephone line queried the relevance of some of the information, wanted it given different priority, and wished to negotiate better procedures. A good deal of adjustment had to take place in information-handling procedures between the early-warning stations and the direction center. To rule out cooperation between early-warning stations and the center was arbitrary and artificial. But, by helping to determine what information should be forwarded to the center, the experimenters would become, in effect, part of the organization being studied.

The early-warning stations had to be considered an integral part of the direction center organization if the laboratory organization were to have all the freedom available to its real-life counterpart.

The first step in the Casey experiment was to add three early-warning stations, each to be operated by a single man. New presentation devices had to be built, the communication net revised, and the design and preparation of input information entirely revamped. In already cramped quarters, space for the early-warning stations had to be shared with a conference room: during operations walls folded out, ceilings slid, and three stations were activated; during post-problem discussions, the early-warning stations were pushed back into the woodwork.

For the Cowboy experiment, when we realized that one-man early-warning stations did not adequately simulate real life, additional communication facilities and more men were provided. (And a larger crew was required.)

"embedding" organizations

There were no adjacent direction centers for the Casey center to co-operate with, as there are in real life, nor a higher headquarters for it to report to. On one occasion, for example, an incoming plane had been identified as hostile by an interceptor pilot who had exhausted his ammunition on another enemy bomber. The Casey center had no other interceptors available and was powerless to oppose the attack. Because it operated in almost complete isolation, it could not even warn civilians in the target area to seek shelter.

The organizations that represented the center's contact with the "rest of the world" had to be provided in some form, just as it had been necessary to use more realistic early-warning stations.

Beginning with the Cowboy experiment, members of the experimental staff represented both an adjacent direction center and the control center at division headquarters. During the Cobra experiment these embedding organizations were manned by more experimenters and had more information and communication facilities for responding realistically, without assuming any responsibility for decisions affecting the defense of the Casey area.

SIMULATING THE CULTURAL ENVIRONMENT

A direction center's culture is a military one. Although we made some attempts to engender a military culture for the college students of the Casey crew, we were not very successful.

The most direct way of dealing with this problem, we decided, was to find a group that had the desired culture and bring it—and the culture—to the laboratory. The Cowboy crew, which was drawn from air-defense installations of the Western Air Defense Force, did bring a more military culture to the laboratory. Experimenters maintained strict social isolation from the crew. (An officer, not a part of the operating crew, was assigned to take care of the crew's administrative problems—pay and per diem records, sick call arrangements, and travel orders.) But in spite of—or perhaps because of—the awkwardness of these precautions, we somehow managed to dilute the "operational atmosphere" with a mysterious "air of experimentation."

So in the next experiment, we communicated with the crew—even for experimental reasons—solely in the name, form and style of the Air Force. (Several of our staff, it turned out, had spent the war years writing Air Force publications.) We prepared a *laboratory* series of division regulations, memoranda and special orders. And although our efforts seemed somewhat elliptical on occasion (not entirely rare for any culture that formalizes its communications), we managed to preserve a more realistic military culture.

leadership

During the training period of the Casey experiment, crew members were rotated through all positions in the organization in an attempt to obtain results that were uncontaminated by a particular leader's style. But the formal leader of the moment could not seem to accept responsibility for establishing long-range policies. Nor did the crew seem to know what to expect from its official leader of the moment. A certain lack of stability resulted—discontinuities in patterns of development. So, prior to the experiment itself, we assigned men of "good" leadership potential to key positions to promote organizational stability and development.

Only the five officers of the Cowboy crew could fill the key positions. We reserved the option of selecting one of them for the senior director job, but this gave us few alternatives for choosing a "good" leader. In Cobra and Cogwheel, we relinquished even the freedom to pick a senior director from among the officers; at the time crew members were ordered to duty at RAND, the Air Force designated a senior director who made all other assignments.

But what might have been lost in less than "optimum" leadership, seemed to have been made up in the stronger inclination of the crews to develop on their own under stable leadership.

Here was an experimental procedure that threatened the integrity of the cultural environment; the research plan had to be modified even though this meant sacrifice of experimental control of individual differences in leadership.

motivation

Everybody talks about man's motivation but nobody seems to be able to do much about it. When animals are used in learning experiments, they are frequently put on deprivation diets to standardize their drive to learn responses rewarded with food. Mild starvation is not so much a method for increasing the animals' interest in performing (although this is part of it) but for obtaining somewhat equivalent motivation in each subject. To control man's motivation requires more than overcoming the mores against starving him. Man, as often as not, is moved by abstract ideas—love, truth, patriotism. To harness the power of his most earnest efforts, greater rewards than food, money or even personal survival must be provided.

Our rationale for motivating the crew was: tap intense motivation with the value for defending our country from enemy bombs, reinforce task achievement and only that, maintain realism to warrant continued involvement.

These men, the three military crews and the college students, cherished the value of "defense" as dearly as the rest of us, and perhaps more. But the bright and shining ideal can be tarnished by the vicissitudes of everyday life. We were not averse to refreshing the value. We told them how important the value was—not "just the facts, ma'am," but with as much dramatic impact as we could muster.

Reinforcement is strongly linked to motivation. (In fact, some learning theorists cannot separate them.) To harness the crew's learning capacity—empowered by its motivation to "defend," we had to reinforce in corresponding terms. So we assiduously avoided reinforcing anything but how well it defended its area. The results fed back to the crew never referred to any disparities between its behavior and "standard operating procedures" or any other cultural norms. . . .

SIMULATING THE TASK ENVIRONMENT

The task environment was the independent variable in all four experiments. We had not only the problem of how to design it but also that of how to control its detailed preparation so that the system inputs expressed the design.

the experimental design

In Casey, the experiment using college students, task difficulty was designed to remain level, so to speak. The number of aircraft in the direction center's area was comparable to that of presentday, real-world, peacetime air traffic. Variations in task load were balanced over the entire experiment.

This design was based on the prediction that a given range of difficulty used throughout the experiment would continue to challenge the crew and that learning would result in gradual improvement in performance. But this prediction proved to be woefully inaccurate. The range of task difficulty was indeed stressful—for the first few problems. After this, however, the problems were not difficult at all. In fact, the organization learned its way right out of the experiment. Within a couple of days the college students were maintaining highly effective defense of their area while playing word games and doing homework on the side.

We realized that task difficulty was not the number of aircraft in the area but was instead the difference between the number of aircraft and the crew's load-carrying capacity of the moment: the traffic load that was difficult to handle today might prove quite easy a week from now.

This insight led to a radical alteration of the design for Cowboy. We had to estimate how fast the crew would learn in order to increase task difficulty fast enough to continue to challenge it but not so fast that the task would be too difficult.

In the Cowboy experiment, task load was designed to increase in a series of steps. (The same design was also used for Cobra; Cogwheel, being shorter, used problems selected from the Cowboy-Cobra design.) The design divided the experiment into 64 "periods," each 100 minutes long. The 64 periods were grouped into four "sets" of 16 consecutive periods each; each set was subdivided into four "days" of four periods each. Task load was stepped up from set to set.

The task environment for a period was specified by two groups of variables: one, the kind and number of unknown and hostile aircraft; the other, the characteristics of the friendly traffic from which the critical flights had to be distinguished. These variables and some of their interactions were provided for in a Latin-square design.

preparing the task environment

There were eight radarscopes for which inputs had to be simulated. Sheets of paper with marks on them represented the information from a single rotation of the radar sweep. Each 100 minute period required 1600 such sheets, and in addition, about 80 teletype messages. Thus, throughout the 180-odd hours of an experiment, information about the task environment came to the system at the rate of some 300 symbols a minute and was complex enough to keep a 40-man organization busy.

Each situation presented to the crews was built up of realistic flights combined into traffic patterns that matched the real ones statistically. First, the essential characteristics of a large number of aircraft flights were specified—some 800, in fact. (And included at the outset some planes that flew right through mountains and some aircraft types that have yet to fly.) Then from 1500 hours of calculations, electronic computers produced, on 80,000 punched cards, all the information about each flight for each radar station, taking into account the characteristics of radar equipment, the station's location and surrounding geography.

The number and kind of flights necessary to satisfy the conditions of the experimental design were selected, then the machines assembled all the information about these flights from the track library and produced the actual inputs for each experimental period. A typical period of 100 minutes required about 10,000 cards and took 25 machine-hours to process.

RAND's computing department provided the facilities and know-how for incorporating all manner of special detail, and most important, for insuring quality control of the simulated system inputs.

The first experiment required a four-hour task environment only every other day. While this schedule was met, it is more honest to report we never had more than two hours to spare before an experimental session, and still more honest to say that we drew on the resources and good will of RAND's computing department until there was little left of either.

It is worth noting that the experimental and computing staffs, like the air-defense crews, also indulged in some procedural innovations. The inputs for a two-hour problem initially took three weeks, seven days a week, three shifts a day to prepare. The state of the art now, machine-wise and procedure-wise, permits a similar job to be done in about 10 minutes.

DATA COLLECTION

"Give a man a phone and he'll talk." This characterizes a good deal of an air-defense crew's behavior—it's verbal. Information about the air traffic is passed from man to man by telephone and in face-to-face conversations. In the Casey experiment 18 recorders ran simultaneously to collect these data. Even with increased efficiency in their use (having to do with tapping into the telephone net at more advantageous places), 22 recorders were required for the subsequent experiments.

In addition to these recordings, we began, in the Cowboy experiment, to record communication patterns by punching, every 15 seconds, a card which showed the telephone lines in use. And in the Cobra experiment we took pictures of the main plotting board every minute.

But a crew does more than just talk. We have tried activity analysis, periodic samplings of gross movements within the station, the collection of "organizational incidents" and other techniques. For observers to penetrate, with the naked eye, the devious machinations of a growing organization, to translate behavior into meaningful codes, and to maintain a standard set over the entire experiment is a data collection problem that can only be described as horrid.

We also obtained information before and after the experiment. Beginning with Casey, we got individual test scores and did individual and group interviews following the run. Then we gradually added to our post-experimental explorations so that after the Cobra experiment these probings took a full week and included an extensive interview program, sociometric and attitude questionnaires, one of R. F. Bales' standard discussion situations, and psychodrama sessions.

Improvements in data collection led to better recordings and record keeping and to more comprehensive information about operations and the individuals who made up the crews. These efforts at completeness also meant that in sheer volume the data were overwhelming. By the end of the four experiments more than 12,000 hours of recordings, and other descriptive material, had been crowded into 60 file drawers. With this much data, proper filing becomes as critical as the techniques of collecting it; an unidentified recording can be even more devastating than a noisy one.

DATA PROCESSING

Soon after the beginning of the Casey experiment, we began the process of getting the data off the records. At first verbatim transcriptions from the recordings were done; the transcriptions were then coded. A little later, the codes were revised and data processing was begun anew.

Coding of the Cowboy data was done directly from the records without intervening transcriptions. A sampling method was used to check coding quality.

The next major step was mechanization. By means of special keyboards the Cobra crew's behavior was coded on cards as it took place. This meant that the report of results for the crew could be prepared from a complete tabulation of its handling of the task.

These improvements led to a saving in data reduction costs. The production staff was able to code the verbal behavior of Cogwheel, the last experiment, into scores ready for analysis about four times as fast as it took to reduce Casey data to comparable form. Some twelve steps were involved in reducing the Casey data; the Cogwheel data took only three. And even with this significant saving, more content and better quality was obtained with the Cogwheel codes.

We collected as much data about the crews and their behavior as we could because we were searching for a framework rather than testing a hypothesis. Only part of the data has been successfully coded or explored at any length although literally hundreds of very pretty hypotheses have been lost in it. Although much of this data has been used only to explain specific incidents, it should prove of more general value once we know the appropriate questions to ask of it.

GENERAL FINDINGS

The objective—that of getting organizational behavior into the laboratory—was realized. Each of the four crews gradually came to behave as if it were in a real-life situation. Crew members became deeply involved with the organization's goal and its successes and failures. During enemy attacks, the noise level in the station rose, men came to their feet, and the excitement was obvious. Crew members reported restless nights and bad dreams—attackers boring in without an interceptor available. On one occasion, an officer slipped while stepping off a dais and broke his leg. We were not aware of this event for some ten minutes because there was no perturbation in the crew's activity during the attack in progress. He was back the next day, cast and all, because, as he said, they couldn't get along without him.

The members of each crew became an integral unit in which many interdependencies and co-ordinating skills developed. And each crew learned to perform more effectively. This learning showed itself in procedural shortcuts, reassignment of functions, and increased motor skill to do the job faster and more accurately.

We believe that the "debriefings" following each session, where the operating results were reviewed, were crucial to the learning that led to improved performance. But we have been unable to relate the content of these discussions directly to crew development. Procedures were frequently changed without any sign that an operating problem had been recognized or a solution proposed. As a matter of fact, procedural changes sometimes moved in one direction while discussions went in another. . . .

As crews were confronted by increasingly difficult tasks, they questioned the organization's goal ("the best defense is a good offense"), the adequacy of their equipment ("the grease pencils are no damn good"), the competence of their own members ("Lt. Blank doesn't know what he's doing"), and registered many signs of bad morale. But these seemed to be symptoms of stress—tension release—that were followed by procedural changes. Bad morale may not always be an omen of impending failure inasmuch as even these four "good" crews exhibited such symptoms in the course of their development.

Crews continued to operate very effectively though the task load increased threefold. The most obvious thing crews learned was to distinguish between information useful for task accomplishment and that which was not. Crews focused their attention on important classes of tracks at the expense of unimportant classes.

In addition to dropping many unimportant events from consideration, they adopted short cuts in response to important tracks as well. While effort spent on unimportant tracks decreased markedly, effort devoted to important tracks also declined.

As the task load increased, the crews were caught between two stresses—failure stress and discomfort stress. The first of these arises from the disparity between aspiration and performance; the second from the difference between the effort demanded by the task and that which can be comfortably afforded. The discomfort stress forces discriminations and shortcuts in response; the failure stress guides the gradual acquisition of shortcuts that do not degrade effectiveness.

To characterize an air-defense organization's adaptation as that of separating the important from the unimportant is simplicity itself. But the process is far from simple: a description of a crew's rules of operation, with all contingencies and qualifications expressed, would occupy volumes. Consistency of organizational response is hard to come by when jobs pass from man to man and when the task situation varies. When the traffic load distribution shifts, the crews use redundancy in information input to rebalance the processing load. That redundancy is also the basis for cross checks that insure control of processing performance.

When a crew depends on expected information patterns in its task environment, it becomes sensitive to changes in those patterns. And when it has explored many processing procedures, it becomes aware of action alternatives. Together, sensitivity to information patterns and awareness of action alternatives contribute to oragnizational adaptive potential.

That was our hope. And it is our impression that in none of the experiments had we exhausted the crew's capability to develop finer discriminations and more effective responses to handle heavier and more difficult task situations.

ADDING IT UP

The simplest way of summarizing the incidents, impressions and data of the air-defense experiments is to say that the four organizations behaved like organisms. Not only did the experiments provide graphic demonstrations of how much performance difference resulted from learning, but they also showed how differently the same people used the same tools under essentially the same load conditions at different times. The structures and procedures that glued functional components together so changed that an organization was only nominally the same from day to day. The direction center profited from its experience to grow and adapt like a living organism.

But what does that conclusion imply for organizations other than the laboratory direction center? So far as we are concerned, the ideal organization would be one that bends to current circumstances (preferably anticipated future ones), takes advantage of chance events, makes capital of its competitors'—and its own—mistakes, and indulges in strategic and tactical innovations.

Stated positively, the organization problem seems to us that of designing and managing for operational flexibility. But is this not a well-endorsed objective, sought after by most planners, designers, and managers?

No, it is not.

Take, for instance, the trend towards the design of fixed-procedure systems that gains ultimate expression in automation. Even though fixed procedures might be appropriate for stable task conditions, the designer can still err in either of two directions: if he underestimates task conditions, the system will fail when its data-processing capacity is exceeded; if he overestimates task conditions, a resource cost much greater than that required will be incurred. And the manager can err similarly by prescribing and enforcing what seem to him to be ideal structures and standard procedures. At this point, one can only guess which of presentday military and industrial systems err in one direction and which in the other.

What, then, is to be done to get operational flexibility? To pump invulnerability and efficiency into an organization requires, first of all, the presence in that system of men, and second, conditions to encourage man's capacity to adapt his actions, and the use of his tools, to the immediate situation.

Our research indicates that these are the conditions necessary to promote organizational learning: clarifying the goal, giving the organization as a whole experience with tasks of increasing difficulty, and providing immediate knowledge of results.

But implementing these conditions is a perfectly miserable problem. The proper goal can be extremely hard to determine, performance even harder to measure, the effects of today's actions perhaps not reflected for years, and control of task conditions almost impossible to attain.

Simulation as a technique—in the absence of other stimulating vistas—is promising. It offers, for example, at least a feasible method for building organizational potential artificially when the price of failure in the real world while learning is prohibitive (the system training program for the Air-Defense Command). It also provides a means for eliciting organizational behavior under controlled conditions so that a search may be made for a framework for comprehending organizations.

But if the organism concept is a key insight, what research remains to be done? Unfortunately, by identifying the problem of predicting organization performance as similar to that of predicting the behavior of individual men, rats and pigeons, we have not resolved the enigma. We have only located a few commonsense precautions. We would not, for instance, compare the single-wing to the T-formation by having seventh graders play the Los Angeles Rams. Experience there, we all recognize, makes a difference. And the result might be quite the opposite ten years from now.

Even if we could expect men to learn to deal with significant patterns rather than noise, what are those patterns in the information input to a mail-order house, to the executive suite of a large corporation, to the communications center of the Army Division? Two stresses—failure and discomfort—guided the direction center's learning. Are there third and fourth sources of stress besides? The direction center was able to acquire discriminations at a certain rate. What are the comparable characteristics of the learning process for organizations in more complex environments?

What we have done here is to try to communicate the excitement of what we felt was proximity to a scientific breakthrough on a crucial problem of the present day. As of now the matter rests as a set of substantive and methodological insights in need of extension.

glossary

Analog computer: An analog computer is one which operates with physical quantities, such as water or electric currents, rather than with digits and mathematical symbols. See DIGITAL COMPUTER.

Computer: A computer is a device capable of employing operations that manipulate objects or symbols. It is able to take in information, perform a variety of operations on the data it is given, and then feed out a solution.

Digital computer: A digital computer is a computing device which operates with digits or symbols, rather than with physical quantities. See ANALOG COMPUTER.

Experiment: An experiment is an arrangement of conditions under which a phenomenon to be studied will take place, with a view to ascertaining the influences of these conditions on that phenomenon.

Gaming: Gaming is a particular type of simulation involving the use of human decision-makers in the simulation of a real-life situation which concerns conflicting interests.

Heuristic: Heuristic refers to an object or process that leads to further discovery or conclusions without providing proof of the correctness of the outcome.

Man-machine simulation: Man-machine simulation is simulation in which both calculating machines and human decision-makers interact in simulating a process or system. See PURE-MACHINE SIMULATION.

Mathematical model: A mathematical model is one in which the properties and interactions of the real object or system are abstracted by measurement and expressed as a set of mathematical equations.

Model: A model is a representation of a real object or process, generally constructed in some other form, size, and/or substance.

Monte Carlo method: The Monte Carlo method is a technique for introducing data of a random or probabilistic nature into a model.

Operating model: Operating models are representations of behaving systems that attempt to reproduce its processes in action.

Parameter: A parameter is a quantity in a system or operating model to which the experimenter may assign arbitrary values.

Process: Process is change or activity in an organism or system over time.

Pure-machine simulation: Pure-machine simulation refers to those simulations that are carried out solely by machines. This is in contrast to man-machine or all-man simulation in which human decision-makers serve as part of the model. See MAN-MACHINE SIMULATION.

Real-time simulation: Real-time simulation is a simulation exercise in which the operations in the simulated system are of the same duration as those in the real system which is being simulated. This is in contrast to simulations in which the real time or duration of operations is expanded or compressed.

Simulation: Simulation is the construction and manipulation of an operating model of a behaving system or process.

Stochastic: Stochastic refers to a process or series of events for which the estimate of the probability of a certain outcome approaches true probability as the number of events increases.

System: A system is an integrated group of interacting elements designed to perform jointly a specified function.

Theory of games: The theory of games of "game theory" refers to a branch of mathematical analysis developed by von Neumann and Morgenstern to study tactical and decision-making problems in conflict situations.

Variable: A variable is a quantity that may increase or decrease without other essential change.

a selected and classified bibliography on simulation in the social sciences

I. GENERAL THEORY

Conway, R. W., B. M. Johnson, and W. L. Maxwell, "Some Problems of Digital Systems Simulation," *Management Science,* VI (1959), 92-110.

Geisler, M. A., "Development of Man-Machine Simulation Techniques," The RAND Corporation, P-1945, March 17, 1960.

————, "Integration of Modelling and Simulation in Organizational Studies," The RAND Corporation, P-1634, March 11, 1959.

Goode, H. H., "Simulation—Its Place in System Design," *Proceedings of International Radio Engineers,* 39 (1951).

McCracken, Daniel D., "The Monte Carlo Method," *Scientific American,* 192 (1955), 90-96.

Malcolm, D. G. (ed.), *Report of System Simulation Symposium.* Baltimore: Waverly Press, Inc., 1957.

Marshall, A. W., "Experimentation by Simulation and Monte Carlo," The RAND Corporation, P-1174, January 28, 1958.

Shubik, Martin, "Bibliography on Simulation, Gaming, Artificial Intelligence and Allied Topics," *Journal American Statistical Association,* 55 (1960), 736-751.

II. SIMULATION IN MILITARY OPERATIONS

Geisler, M. A., "The Simulation of a Large-Scale Military Activity," *Management Science,* V (1959), 359-368.

Kahn, H., and I. Mann, "War Gaming," The RAND Corporation, P-1167, July 30, 1957.

Rowan, T. C., "Simulation in Air Force System Training," in *Report of System Simulation Symposium,* D. G. Malcolm (ed.). Baltimore: Waverly Press, Inc., 1958.

III. INDUSTRIAL ENGINEERING

Brotman, L., and J. Minker, "Digital Simulation of Complex Traffic Problems in Communication Systems," *Operations Research*, V (1957), 670-679.

Floody, J. J., and R. J. A. Paul, "Simulation Techniques in Aeronautics," *Journal of the Royal Aeronautical Society*, 62 (1958).

Hurd, C. C., "Simulation by Computation as an Operations Research Tool," *Operations Research*, II (1954), 205-207.

Jackson, J. R., "Simulation Research on Job Shop Production," *Naval Research Log. Quart.*, IV (1957), 287-295.

IV. ECONOMICS AND BUSINESS SIMULATION

Cohen, Kalman J., and Eric Rhenman, "The Role of Management Games in Education and Research," *Management Science*, VII (1961), 131-166.

Greenlaw, Paul S., Lowell W. Herron, and Richard H. Rawdon, *Business Simulation: In Industrial and University Education*. Englewood Cliffs, N.J.: Prentice-Hall, Inc., 1962.

Martin, E. W., Jr., "Simulation in Organizational Research," *Business Horizons*, II (1959), 68-77.

Orcutt, Guy H., M. Greenberger, J. Korbel, and A. Rivlin. *Microanalysis of Socioeconomic Systems: A Simulation Study*. New York: Harper & Brothers, 1961.

Shubik, Martin, "Simulation of Industry and Firm," *American Economic Review*, L (1960), 908-919.

Vance, Stanley, *Management Decision Simulation*. New York: McGraw-Hill, Inc., 1960.

V. PSYCHOLOGY

Gagne, R. M., "Training Devices and Simulators: Some Research Issues," *American Psychologist*, IX (1954), 95-107.

Mahler, W. R., and G. K. Bennett, *Psychological Studies of Advanced Naval Training: Evaluation of Flight Trainers*. Port Washington: USN Training Devices Center, 1950. Technical Report SDC 999-1-1.

Newell, A., J. C. Shaw, and H. A. Simon, "Elements of a Theory of Human Problem Solving," *Psychological Review*, 65 (1958), 151-166.

Reitman, Walter R., "Heuristic Programs, Computer Simulation, and Higher Mental Process," *Behavioral Science*, IV (1959), 330-335.

VI. POLITICAL SCIENCE

Bloomfield, L. P., and Norman Padelford, "Three Experiments in Political Gaming," *American Political Science Review,* 53 (1959), 1105-1115.

Goldhamer, Herbert, and Hans Speier, "Some Observations on Political Gaming," *World Politics,* 12 (1959), 71-83.

Morgan, Thomas B., "The People-Machine," *Harper's,* 222 (1961), 53-57.

VII. SOCIOLOGY

Guetzkow, Harold, and A. E. Bowes, "The Development of Organizations in a Laboratory," *Management Science,* III (1957), 380-402.

Meier, Richard L., "Explorations in the Realm of Organization Theory. IV: The Simulation of Social Organizations," *Behavioral Science,* VI (1961), 232-248.

Rome, Sydney C., and Beatrice K. Rome, "The Leviathan Technique for Large-Group Analysis," *Behavioral Science,* VI (1961), 148-152.

index

Prepared by Larry A. Eberhardt